GROUP ACTIVITIES
with Older Adults

Vicki Dent

Speechmark (S

Speechmark Publishing Ltd
Telford Road, Bicester, Oxon OX26 4LQ, UK

DEDICATION

I would like to dedicate this book to my husband Lee, whose never-ending support and understanding makes everything possible and to my son Joshua who makes everything complete.

Published by

Speechmark Publishing Ltd, Telford Road, Bicester, Oxon OX26 4LQ, UK

Telephone: +44 (0) 1869 244 644   Fax: +44 (0) 1869 320 040

www.speechmark.net

© Vicki Dent, 2003
Reprinted 2004

002-5096/Printed in the United Kingdom/2090

British Library Cataloguing in Publication Data

Dent, Vicki
   Group activities with older adults
   1. Recreational therapy for the aged   2. Group games   3. Nursing homes – Recreational activities
   I. Title
   362.6'1

ISBN 0 86388 342 7

Contents

Acknowledgements

In compiling the activities for this book I have drawn on the knowledge and experience that has been shared with me over the years by numerous committed and hardworking activity organisers. The role of Activity Organiser can be one of the hardest to undertake in a care home, but it is one that, in my experience, is usually approached with energy and enthusiasm, a huge sense of fun and an overriding desire to achieve a high quality of life for older people. I thank all of the activity organisers that I have had the pleasure of knowing for making my working roles as enjoyable as they have been.

It is also important to acknowledge two other people who made this book possible: Dr Tessa Perrin, who gave me the encouragement to undertake it in the first place, and Robin Dynes, whose constructive comments helped to give it the shape and focus it has today.

Introduction

More and more residential care homes are beginning to understand the need for effective group activities. This includes the understanding that:

■ Caring for someone completely and holistically requires a consideration of their social and occupational needs, and the opportunity for social activity and interaction.
■ Occupational deprivation – the lack of purposeful, meaningful, valuable activity – has serious consequences on the health of all, no matter their age, illness or disability.
■ The more active an individual remains – mentally and physically – the more skills they are likely to retain for longer, the more independent they can remain, and consequently the better the quality of life they are likely to enjoy.
■ Activity can have a therapeutic and beneficial effect, and can therefore contribute positively to skills maintenance – retaining the ability to do – and rehabilitation – relearning skills that may have been lost.

Consequently more and more care home owners and managers are making arrangements for the provision of group activities. These arrangements include dedicated activity organisers with specific hours to provide activities for residents; dedicated hours for activities, given to care staff as an additional role, and arrangements for external activity organisers to come into the home on a regular basis. Whatever the arrangement, the desire should be the same – to provide an effective group activity programme that meets the needs of the residents.

Providing an effective group activity programme is not simply about filling time – something that can be forgotten or postponed because there is neither the time nor the staff to undertake the activity. Nor is it simply about providing entertainment: activity organisers are not Butlins red coat staff. Activities and activity organisers are an essential part of the care package required by residents in a residential care setting. Human beings are innately active beings – they need to do; to have a part to play and a purpose, to give themselves identity and meaning. While this strongly indicates the need for activity to continue throughout each person's life, it is this statement that generates the difficulties in providing an effective activity programme. An effective programme meets the needs of a group of individuals to be active and to have value and purpose in their lives. However, every individual will have a different perspective of what adds value, meaning and purpose to life.

Successful activity organisers need to learn the art of informed compromise. They need to:

■ Be able to identify the needs of individuals, and then balance these against the needs of the group.
■ Learn how to give quality time to a group or individual balanced against a tight resource of hours.
■ Learn to tap into a range of resources, while balancing this need against a tight (or non-existent) budget.

A key skill to look for when appointing an activity organiser should be the ability to juggle! To assist in this balancing act and compromise, this book aims to look at group activities in detail. Part 1 (Chapters 1–5) explores the issues behind providing effective group activities. Chapter 1 investigates the reasons for having group activities: how they can meet needs and bring about benefits for residents. Chapter 2 reflects on the issues that need to be addressed and the skills that an activity organiser should have to ensure that the group programme is effective. Chapter 3 looks at resource requirements and how these might be met. It addresses the challenge of involving others – staff and families – in activity provision, and also looks at general considerations when programme-planning.

Chapter 4 addresses the needs of different client groups. Most of the book is concerned with activities for older people with nursing and care needs. This chapter explores some of the different activity needs of people with dementia and younger people.

Chapter 5 works through hints, tips and tools for recording the activities offered and participation levels, and will help the activity organiser to demonstrate the effectiveness of their service, as well as aiding evaluation and development of the group programme. Individual needs change, and the activity programme must change and develop with the group that it is aimed at.

In Part 2 (Chapter 6), the specifics of what activities to offer are addressed. The 'ten areas of need' approach is introduced. The remainder of this section gives a step-by-step guide to a range of activities. It covers why such activities should be included in a programme; what benefits they will bring; what resources will be needed to do the activity, and how to run the session. There are also hints and tips on changing the activity, and solving problems and difficulties that might be encountered during an activity.

For anyone tasked with providing group activities for residents of a care home, this book offers:

■ Information and advice on developing an effective activity service
■ Direction in terms of how to plan an activity programme
■ Ideas for activities, and detail on how to organise them
■ Associated information related to evaluation and documentation
■ A sample programme and documentation tools

Part 1

Making **Group** **Activities** Work

Chapter 1 The Benefits of Groups

Social aspect

Groups serve many purposes: the coming together of like-minded individuals to achieve a goal; to share a common interest; to gain support or information; to share ideas or thoughts; to solve a problem; or simply to be.

There will be occasions when residents choose to be in the vicinity of the activity session, without wishing to take an active part. Their needs are to:

- Feel part of the group without having to risk failure, look foolish or be expected to interact or participate
- Enjoy the conversation
- Observe their peers
- Toe-dip the activity as a precursor to becoming more involved on future occasions
- Gather information that they can share with family and friends
- Participate in the group for the social elements only.

For example, the activity organiser might facilitate a knitting circle in a home lounge. Imagine the scene: there is a small group of chairs clustered around a coffee table. Three residents arrive and are seated, leaving an empty chair between each other. Another two arrive and are seated in the same manner. They each have a knitting bag containing some ongoing work. The activity organiser joins them and begins to talk to two of the residents, inviting them to begin their knitting. The session begins. There is much chatter and conversation as the activity organiser works her way around the group, taking a spare seat between two residents each time. The residents start to knit; they do a few stitches, but then encounter a difficulty. They hand their knitting to the activity organiser for her to solve the problem, and once solved she retains each resident's knitting for a short while, knitting furiously while chatting, engaging each person in conversation. Towards the end of the session, the activity organiser goes to fetch refreshments. Later, when asked about their knitting circle, the participants speak warmly of the others and the activity organiser, expressing their enjoyment at being able to spend time with each other, while acknowledging how hard they had to work during the session. For them, the proof is there – they meet weekly to knit; their individual projects are growing and looking wonderful; they are obviously working hard.

Whether they were truly aware that the activity organiser was undertaking the majority of the work was, on this occasion, irrelevant: they were enjoying the very social nature of the activity – being together, with a common goal; a shared interest that had an external value. It must be remembered, of course, that for some residents this session would not have met their needs. If the need had been to produce work independently, no matter the standard, or if the activity organiser had hoped to develop the residents' skills, then an alternative approach would have been required.

Groups provide an opportunity to be with others – preferably people with similar interests or backgrounds. For many this is a pleasant arrangement – being with others. For some, however, the thought of spending time with others is at best unfamiliar, at worst frightening or unwanted. Careful consideration should be given to those whose memory is poor – few people would choose to constantly spend time with strangers, and for those who find it difficult to retain information other residents and often the staff remain strangers. Equally, thought should be given to new residents. Where have they come from? What has been their recent experience? If they have moved to the care home from a hospital ward they may be more comfortable with having others around them. If they have moved from home, they may have been living alone for many years, and may have focused their lives into one or two rooms within their home. A communal setting with 20 or 30 other people will be an extreme that they may not wish to be part of – certainly not initially.

Role definition

Generally, everyone likes to feel they have a part to play, a place where they belong, a role to undertake. Group work provides the opportunity for individuals to undertake one or more of a number of established roles. For example, the information-giver, tutor or leader – a resident who is an experienced traveller could share their information and knowledge with their peers via a slide show or discussion, reinforcing past hobbies and interests, validating their knowledge and their own sense of self worth and value. The parent, spouse, carer, or giver role can be encouraged in the more able residents who could assist those less able, sitting with them, helping them to undertake the activity, writing down answers for them. Residents who continue to enjoy 'doing' can have their value reinforced through assisting with the session – calling out the numbers at Bingo; asking the questions during a quiz; helping with the tea during a break and so on. The resident who prefers to be 'done for' can sit back and allow others to 'support' them in the manner in which they may have become accustomed!

There will be issues relating to residents undertaking a role: potential conflict when more than one resident wishes to play a certain role, and when other residents may not welcome them undertaking that role. Good communication, awareness and understanding should help overcome these kinds of difficulties, but what of health and safety? There are likely to be risk implications of residents helping out, but it is generally accepted that taking informed risks is good for psychological health and wellbeing. Residents often respond to the unintentional messages that are given out – for example, 'Just have a seat, I'll do that for you', can be perceived as 'you are not capable'. This message of 'you are not capable' combined with the need to move into a care facility, reinforces an individual's difficulties and disabilities. Taking informed risk can reinforce people's abilities, boosting self-esteem and self-worth and psychological wellbeing. Good risk assessment should not be about preventing things from happening, but about anticipating risk and taking the necessary steps to avoid harm and injury. If a resident wishes to help out with the tea trolley, helping to pour the tea carries a high risk; however, passing round the biscuits, collecting up the cups, or helping a member of staff to push the trolley carries less risk, while allowing the resident to retain a sense of being useful and helpful.

Role modelling

As well as providing individuals with an opportunity to undertake a role, groups can provide an ideal opportunity for role modelling – an approach whereby a task is demonstrated for others to follow. This 'demonstration' may be overt – 'copy what I do'. In these circumstances residents will be able to acknowledge that they do not know, or cannot remember how to do something. The activity organiser is then free to lead, guide and actively demonstrate. In many more circumstances, the residents will be unwilling or unable to admit to a lack of memory or lack of knowledge. Then the role modelling should be much more subtle. Residents will often attempt to compensate for difficulties: if they cannot remember how to do something, they will first look around to see what others are doing. Think about some common, anxiety-provoking group-setting situations, for example, having a meal in a restaurant and being unsure of which knife to use, or whether it would be OK in the present company to pick up the chicken and eat it. The solution – look around to see what others are doing. This is a subtle form of role modelling that can enable individuals to retain and sometimes relearn skills without the anxieties of having to admit to difficulties. Cooking, baking, gardening, brass-polishing, laying the tables, folding the laundry – skills that will have been very familiar – may be slipping away. Providing these activities as part of the programme enables an individual to work alongside the activity organiser or another resident, providing them with the opportunity to 'copy' others undertaking those tasks. This will go some way towards ensuring a 'failure free' activity, leaving the resident feeling positive about the activity experience.

Partnership approach

Working in a group can provide the opportunity for partnership – partnership between all members, whether staff, families or residents. The sayings go 'Two heads are better than one' and 'Many hands make light work'. At times when an individual would perhaps struggle to undertake an activity independently, working with another might facilitate success. As with all activity-planning, successful partnerships need careful thought and consideration. Knowledge of the group members should help in identifying the skills and strengths of individuals, and through careful matching, these strengths can be pooled to ensure failure-free outcomes.

The key skill essential to ensuring a successful partnership approach is being able to identify the component parts of an activity, and then matching the parts to the skills and abilities of the individuals who wish to participate.

For example, flower arranging. What are the component parts? Gaining an overall understanding of the task in hand; selecting a receptacle for the arrangement; selecting a range and variety of flowers and greenery; cutting, trimming and placing the flowers in the receptacle, and then deciding on where to display and how to maintain the arrangement. Knowledge of the individuals within the group will identify those who have the cognitive ability to fully understand the task in hand; those who have the physical strength and dexterity to cut, trim and place the flowers; those who have the creative flair for selecting the colours, variety and style of flowers that make an effective arrangement. Some of the residents may be able to undertake this activity independently; others will need a partnership approach. By allocating each individual a role to play based on their strengths – somebody to select the flowers; somebody else to cut and trim; another person to arrange the display – the group can achieve, through partnership, a successful outcome.

As with all activities, there may be problems along the way – in particular the resident who does not see the need for a partner; who feels able to undertake the activity independently, despite limited abilities. On these occasions, knowledge of the individual involved will be essential. How important is the finished article likely to be to that individual? Often the taking part – being involved in the process – is much more important than the finished article. Are they likely to be able to achieve a finished article that is of an acceptable standard to them? If yes, then there is no problem. If no, consider how best to support them so that they can work independently and achieve the finish that they will find acceptable. There is no easy answer to this one: the activity organiser may be able to help along the way, perhaps making subtle adjustments after the session has finished. Alternatively, this may be an activity that is not suitable or appropriate for the resident to participate in, due to the risk of disappointment that they may face.

When not to use groups

For many residents, group activities will be a successful route to active involvement and engagement within the community of the care facility; however, for a small number of individuals, group activities pose a large threat to their sense of wellbeing. As mentioned above, residents may well have spent many years alone, with few friends or family. They may have naturally shied away from communal events and overt socialisation. Their recent life experience may have been limited to activities within their own home – watching television, reading, receiving an occasional visitor. Obviously, it is difficult to generalise about people's response to the change in environment: for some, there may be huge interest in attending activities; doing things that they have been unable to do; being able to spend time with others. For others, the idea of attending group activities in large communal spaces, often at some distance from their room, may be at best anxiety-provoking, at worst threatening. For these people, a 'softly softly' approach may be successful – ensuring that the individual is aware of the activities on offer, without pressuring them to join in. They may become aware of the enjoyment that participating can bring through discussion with others; through seeing the evidence of activities – work that has been produced; hearing music and laughter coming from the lounge; viewing photographs that have been taken of activities in progress. The key to the 'softly softly' approach is to stay in touch with the resident; acknowledge their anxieties; keep them informed; keep open their option to attend, while always respecting their choice not to attend.

Knowledge of the individuals within the home may identify residents, or more likely a combination of residents, who when brought together will cause distress, upset and angry confrontation. Differing abilities and difficulties can cause frustration. For example:

- The lady who wants to attend the church service, but insists on shouting throughout, may cause upset to others attending.
- The gentleman who likes to call out the Bingo numbers but does so too fast (or too slowly) for the liking of those playing. Different perceptions of the way things should be done can cause frustration and anger.
- The dominoes player who insists on certain rules that are unfamiliar to other players.
- The retired fitness instructor who dislikes music being played during an exercise session, because 'exercise should be taken seriously!'

These are all possible scenarios that challenge the group approach. The answer, as always, is never easy. Here are some questions to help think the situation through:

- Is there the option of running sessions twice, aimed at different ability levels, in different styles?
- Is it possible to sit down with the resident whose behaviour is causing upset to others, to talk through the problem and come up with a solution?
- Should the individual be excluded from certain activities?
- Are there alternative activities, or perhaps roles within the activity, that may divert from the problem?
- Is there someone who might be able to join the group to support certain residents, thereby enabling them to participate fully without causing disruption?

Needs of the individual

Having looked at the difficulties that can occur through participating in groups, it becomes apparent that there will be residents for whom group activities are not a feasible option, and for whom an individual approach is required. This can be time-consuming, so careful thought is needed. Having identified the residents who need one-to-one input, try to identify the kind of individual activities that they would enjoy – one-to-one does not have to be simply chatting to people. Card games, dominoes, board games, crosswords, reading the newspaper, taking a walk, receiving communion, reading the Bible, listening to music, receiving a hand massage (to name just a few), are all activities that can be offered on a one-to-one basis. Having identified the activities that the resident would like to participate in, think about the frequency of input required: some may need one-to-one time every day;

others may be content with weekly or monthly sessions. This will be very dependent on their ability to meet their own activity needs, and the access that they have to others – family and friends, for example. Having identified the kind and frequency of one-to-one activities required, these sessions should be planned into the programme in the same way that group activities are planned.

As previously mentioned, individual input is time-consuming, so try to identify alternative resources available to provide individual activities – volunteers, other staff, friends and family, other residents, or perhaps external community groups. There will always be a very small, core group of residents who will make an active and valid choice to decline all or most group activities. Their wishes should be respected; however, for the other residents, try to view individual time as a way of encouraging residents to take an interest in group work, so that one-to-one input becomes a temporary arrangement rather than a permanent one.

Chapter 2 Ensuring Group Effectiveness

Assessment

A group programme will be only as effective as the assessment it is based on. In Chapter 1, a number of references were made to the importance of knowing the residents. This should be obvious, for how can a programme be planned without knowing what the residents want and need? Many activity organisers rely on 'gut instinct' – they have got to know their resident group over a period of time, and feel comfortable that they know what activities will work and what will not. That is fine, but what if the activity organiser is new to the home and new to activities? That familiarity with the residents does not exist. In an ideal world, a new activity organiser should be able to make reference to existing assessments. In reality, many homes are still only beginning to recruit activity organisers, and there are therefore no previous records to refer to. For those that have had activity organisers, few assessments are ever recorded: few 'gut instincts' are documented.

So what should be included in an assessment? An assessment is a tool for finding out. Therefore, the starting point for any assessment process should be 'What do you want to find out?' In activities, relevant information is likely to fall under five main headings:

- What the individual wants to do
- What the individual needs to do
- What the individual is capable of doing
- The level of support that may be required to aid achievement
- Additional information, such as previous interests and hobbies; personal preferences and values; useful and pertinent background information.

Having established the information to be collected, the method – or usually methods – for gathering that information needs to be identified. A form and an assessment sheet to highlight the information required is ideal (see Appendix 1 for an example). Contact the people who have the information to fill in the details – the resident, the resident's family and friends (particularly important when the resident is unable to communicate the information for themselves), and other staff.

Having found out the information and recorded it (for reference now and in the future) – lay out a baseline – a starting point for comparison. Ensure that the record is kept as accurate and up to date as possible. An assessment is not a one-off process to be completed on admission. It is an ongoing document that should be added to as more is learned about the resident, as abilities, likes and dislikes change. Others should be able to refer to the assessment record and be aware of as current a picture as is possible. Finally, ensure that the information gathered is used. Develop a profile of the resident group – a list of people with similar likes and dislikes; highlight the range of activities in which they have expressed an interest; identify the range of abilities and support needed. Use this information to develop the group programme.

A few words of caution in relation to keeping records: the information that is collected on an individual belongs to the individual it pertains to. This information is confidential. As far as possible, ensure that the individual is aware of what the information is being collected for, where it will be stored, and who will have access to it. They may choose not to share information given, and their wishes must be respected. Any document that relates to a resident can be classified as a legal document. Ensure that records are completed in line with organisational policy. This is likely to include:

- Documentation to be completed in ink – usually blue or black.
- Entries to be legibly signed and dated by the person making the record.
- Entries must contain fact. Any opinions or subjective statements should be recorded as such – for example, 'In my opinion, Mrs Jones would benefit from attending group activities.', 'I believe that Mrs Jones would find the quiz session too distressing to attend.'

Assessing the needs and wants of the resident group will highlight the activities to offer, and this is covered in more detail in later chapters. However, there are other things to be considered to ensure effectiveness of the group programme, and these are covered below.

Timings

When planning the programme, consider the timings for different activities. There are likely to be three prime activity times in a day – a session in the morning, in the afternoon, and in the evening. Every care facility has different timings, but generally a similar routine. The morning is often dominated by personal care-based activities; residents will arise at different times, and they will have breakfast at different times. Many homes find that residents are more alert in the mornings (probably due to the amount of stimulation that they receive), but their availability to join a large group activity is limited. This would suggest that the morning session is better suited to individual activities, small group activities, or activities that residents can join as they are available. For example, poetry reading, discussion sessions, handicraft sessions and sensory sessions, to name a few. As the morning progresses and lunchtime approaches, it is often the case that more residents are around in preparation for entering the dining area. This time is well suited to bringing residents up to date with the day; informing them of the afternoon's activities, and perhaps catching up with the news of the day, with a glass of sherry to stimulate the appetite.

After lunch, it would appear that homes generally find their residents fall into one of two categories: those who like to have a nap after their meal, and those who are ready to go straight into an afternoon of activity. The afternoon session has the potential for being the longest prime-time slot of the day – often up to three hours long. For many residents, limited attention span and poor concentration levels prevent very long activity sessions, so little and often becomes the order of the day. This would suggest that a varied programme could be planned for the afternoon, each session lasting approximately 45 minutes, which would enable those who do not need a rest to go into all sessions, and those who wish or need to take a rest to do so before or between sessions. They could then join the session and a new activity later in the afternoon. There will also be occasions when an activity might require a longer session – an entertainer, for example – and the afternoon would suggest itself as the most appropriate time.

The final prime time is the evening. It is the authors' experience that fewer residents are interested in regular evening activities, wishing to retire early, or to take advantage of the generally quieter time for peace and reflection. However, offering the occasional evening activity – perhaps monthly – gives variety, and also the opportunity for family members who might be busy during the day to come along and participate if they wish. Again, the nature of the evening might suggest a larger group and more social type activities, such as a quiz night, a themed party, an entertainment evening, or perhaps a fundraising event.

The numbers game: quantity versus quality

As mentioned earlier, an effective group programme requires a certain degree of selection. Bringing together groups of people with different interests and abilities can cause difficulty, and defeats the aim of activities being pleasurable, fun and enjoyable, and a time to feel positive.

Equally, having a large group of people together does not always facilitate a failure-free approach. For certain activities, often described as passive activities, such as listening to music, watching a show, or listening to a speaker, the more the merrier. However, consideration should be given to the needs that are likely to arise during the session. For example, suppose there is an entertainer in the dining room, and 25 residents will attend. During the performance, it is likely that someone will have personal care needs that will require support and assistance. There is likely to be an interval for refreshments. One individual cannot oversee the activity; be there for the visitors; encourage resident involvement; assist with personal needs; and serve refreshments for 25 people in a person-centred and considerate way.

For more active sessions, such as handicrafts, bingo, cooking, or gardening, residents are likely to need support and assistance to participate in the activity and to achieve their required outcome. The numbers attending this kind of session should be reflective of the level of support available to the session. If, as often happens, the activity organiser is left to undertake the activity alone, then the group size should be limited. The number participating should ensure that everyone goes away feeling that they have enjoyed the activity; that they have achieved their preferred outcome, and that they would like to be able to attend again in the future.

Activity analysis

Part of the assessment process refers to gathering information relating to the abilities of the individual. This is not about identifying activities that the resident is unable to do, it is about identifying their strengths. Under 'partnership approach', the skill of breaking down activities into component parts was mentioned. This is known as 'activity analysis', and it requires further and closer consideration.

Activity analysis is a technique used to identify the skills and abilities required to undertake an activity. For a group to be effective, the group leader needs to be fully aware of the skills required to undertake that activity, in order to compare them with the skills of the individuals attending the session. Having identified the skills required, and completed the comparisons, certain decisions can be made. Is it an inappropriate activity for any of the interested individuals – likely to cause too much frustration and distress? Is the activity outside the definition of a challenge? If the answer to these two questions is no, and yet the strengths of the residents are less than the skills required, what next? Is it possible to take a partnership approach to this activity? Is it possible to adapt the activity to enable a resident to participate? The more activities that can be approached from a partnership perspective, and the more activities that can be adapted to fit the skills and abilities of the resident, the more activities a resident will be able to participate in.

For example, if a resident were invited to make a cup of tea, an activity organiser might make a judgement as to how difficult the individual would find that activity, but the detail as to what they might find difficult, and how assistance might be offered to help them achieve the desired outcome, might be less clear. If consideration was given to the component parts, and therefore the skills required in relation to that activity, then this might become clearer. Put simply, to achieve the desired outcome the resident would need to understand the overall task, and the process and steps involved, and be safety aware and have certain physical abilities. Each of these elements could present a difficulty, but each could be adapted to suit the abilities of the resident. If word comprehension (understanding the task) is difficult, use pictures or demonstration. If task comprehension is difficult, advise step by step. If safety awareness is not present, ensure that they are supervised at all times. If physical strength or movement is not present, then use adapted equipment, offer assistance, or undertake that element for them. Table 2.1 gives a full analysis of the activity 'making a cup of tea', in order to illustrate the process further.

So, in summary, the process of activity analysis is:

- Identify the activities in which residents would like to participate
- Analyse those activities to identify the skills and capabilities required
- Compare those to the skills and abilities of the interested residents
- Adapt the activities according to these findings.

Table 2.1 **Activity analysis: making a cup of tea**

Components of the activity	Skills and abilities required	Notes	Adaptations
Understanding instruction	Language comprehension	Imagine being asked to make a cup of tea in an unknown language	Give instructions using pictures, gestures or through demonstration
Following correct order	Ability to sequence	Putting tea-bag into pot or cup before adding water. Boiling kettle before pouring water on to tea-bag	Give each instruction, one at a time Ensure each instruction is completed before giving the next instruction
Filling kettle, plugging in, switching on kettle	Safety awareness Upper limb strength Balance Mobility Fine motor skills: grip and strength	Water and electricity. Use of hot water To hold the kettle while it is filling To stand to fill the kettle at the sink To move around the kitchen area To plug in the kettle and switch it on	Ensure supervision Fill the kettle from a jug Offer a high stool to sit on at the sink Fill the kettle before beginning the task Make use of adapted plugs Undertake certain tasks for them
Awareness of kettle being boiled	Hearing Sight Understanding of the workings of a kettle	To hear any 'boiled' indicator To see steam or light indicator	Offer supervision or prompts
Pouring kettle into cup, mug, or pot	Knowledge of items required Ability to indicate choice Upper limb strength Coordination and stability of movement Sight Safety awareness	To select the correct item To use the item of choice (cup or mug) To lift and tip the kettle To pour the water into the item of choice To see when the item is full To remain safe with hot water	Have a selection of items in sight or within reach Aid choice Use adapted equipment – kettle tipper Supervision
Adding milk, sugar as preferred	Knowledge of the items required Ability to indicate a preference Fine motor skills Grip and wrist movement	To select the correct items To make a drink that is acceptable To manipulate the spoon To manipulate the bottle for pouring	Have milk and sugar in sight or within reach Use large, grip-handled cutlery Use a jug
Drinking	Safety awareness Grip Coordination Swallow reflex	To drink when at the correct temperature To hold the cup or mug To bring the cup or mug to the mouth To swallow the drink	Supervision Use adapted cup or mug

Group dynamics

Having identified the activity programme that the residents want and need, and the best time of the day for the different activities, and having analysed and adapted the sessions to enable a failure-free session, surely it is time to get on and run the activity session? Unfortunately, the difficulties don't stop there. During a group session there will be a whole range of dynamics that the activity organiser should be aware of and try to manage. For example:

■ The resident who likes to dominate the activity by answering all the questions before anyone else.

■ The resident who has a lot to share, but never speaks loud enough for any of the other residents to hear them.

■ The resident who likes to come in late, disturbing everybody else who is already settled.

■ The resident who likes to have the activity organiser's attention to the exclusion of all others.

■ The resident who enjoys joining the activities, but is prone to making incomprehensible noises throughout.

Having an awareness of group dynamics will help the activity organiser understand some of the reasons behind certain behaviours, and may shed light on methods for managing and even solving some of the difficulties.

Whenever a group of people comes together – particularly if they are an unfamiliar group – there is a process that people go through. To function within a group, each individual needs to be clear on their role within the group, and feel comfortable that the other group members are aware of their role. For example, there will be people who feel that it is their role to make things happen – they may naturally be people who like to get things done, get a decision made, and make progress. Likewise, there may be people who like to see how things are going before joining in and offering their contribution; but nevertheless, when the time is right, the contribution will be made. There may be someone who is more reserved – who needs 'persuading' that they have something of value to add to the proceedings – naturally a shy person, not one to push themselves forward into the thick of things. Whatever the role taken, it is likely to be based on the natural personality of the individual. This is not always a conscious awareness: people rarely enter a group session determined to take the lead (except perhaps for an activity organiser!). More often, the behaviours are more subtle, and only become apparent on closer inspection. This is where an understanding of these dynamics – this natural movement into a comfortable role – can help.

Consider again some of the earlier examples, and begin to understand the subconscious message. This will help develop a strategy for managing the differences, and therefore achieving a successful group.

The resident who likes to dominate the activity by answering all the questions before anyone else is likely to be a natural leader. The individual may want to progress the session, get the quiz finished; they are perhaps someone who doesn't like to hang around. Under these circumstances, consider the rest of the group and the nature of the session. If it is a session that requires quick decisions, they may be the ideal people to include. If the session is better run at a more leisurely pace, then it will be necessary to find a way of slowing down this type of individual. Could they have a more difficult activity? Could they be given the role of assisting others? Is it possible to have a discussion with them about allowing other residents to have a chance? They may feel it necessary to show to others that they are alert and intelligent. This could perhaps be tackled by making them question-master.

And what about the resident who has a lot to share, but never speaks loud enough for any of the other residents to hear them? The quietness may be a result of illness or disability. It may be a result of shyness, or a lack of confidence in their ability to make a comment of value. Again, consider the other members of the group. Is it possible to ask them to give additional consideration when this particular individual is speaking? Is there anything that could be done to make sure the quiet resident is heard – perhaps the use of a microphone, or agreeing beforehand that the activity organiser should summarise any points that they make, so that the rest of the residents in the group hear the contributions.

The resident who likes to come in late, disturbing everybody else who is already settled, is often someone who needs to have their value recognised; who likes to be sure that all are aware of their presence, and who may like to take control of situations. By arriving late, it is possible that the activity has to stop, and they can then restart it under their own terms. Is it possible to have a quiet word with this resident, and explain the disruption that they cause? Is this someone who could be given a role, on the understanding that they would need to be there at the outset? Of course, it is possible that the late arrival is for other reasons. Perhaps they need a lot of assistance, are dependant on staff getting them to the session on time, and are concerned themselves at their consistent late arrival. A tactful discussion with staff, highlighting the individual's desire to be at the activity on time, might make a difference.

Above all, try to take a step back during activity sessions to understand the roles that people are trying to take, or are taking, and think about alternatives that enable them to have the role they desire, as well as facilitating the group.

Process versus outcome

When providing group activities, the final element to consider before launching the residents into the session is 'What could this group achieve?' Each activity should have a beginning, middle and an end, and for each activity as well as each individual resident, different elements of that process will have more importance and value than others. For example, a sing-along. The middle of this kind of activity is likely to be the favourite part: singing along to favourites and requesting different songs, whereas the beginning and ending of the session will have less value (unless it is someone who has not enjoyed listening to others singing!). Consider an alternative, a craft session: salt dough, for example. The end product may be the valued part of this activity. Mixing the dough, rolling, moulding, baking, and painting are all necessary activities undertaken to get to the finished piece – something that could be given to relatives or sold at the summer fair.

It is important to be clear about where the value may lie in the activity, and whether this fits with the value placed on the activity by the resident. To explain this further – for some, a beautifully finished item will be the desired outcome, and producing a finished article may be the reason for undertaking the activity, but this may be beyond the individuals' ability level. Assistance could be offered in order to achieve the outcome; however, this may not be desired by, or be acceptable to, the resident – they may wish to be independent. The activity may be a familiar one for them; it may be something that they have undertaken to a high skill level. This may lead to only one alternative – not to participate, due to a wish not to lower personal standards. In this example, the value of the activity is in the finished article for both the activity and the resident, but the skill level of the resident will lead to an unhappy experience.

For others, the outcome will be less important. The resident is perhaps trying something new – something that they have never really been very good at, and therefore any outcome is a success. Alternatively, the activity itself is not leading to an outcome. A consistent message from the activity organiser of 'let's have some fun, let's see how we get on, let's not worry about what it looks like', can lead to an activity where the doing is much more important than the outcome, and people can relax and have a go. On this occasion, the value lies very much in everybody having a go, and the residents themselves are happy to participate on that basis: a recipe for success.

As a general note: when an activity is held for the purpose of enjoying the process rather than worrying about the outcome, ensure that staff and families, for example, are made aware of this approach. Without this awareness, others can inadvertently criticise what they see as poor quality finished pieces, leading to a sense that 'the activity is not worth doing' because of the outcome, or worse still, that the activity is patronising because the outcome is not good enough, despite the fact that everybody had lots of fun participating!

Chapter 3 Planning a Programme

Programme planning

When the time comes to plan the activity programme, there are a number of points worth consideration. The starting point is how 'planned' should the programme be? Is it better to have a structured plan or to be completely flexible, offering the activity that the residents request at the time? The answer is a bit of both. Without planning, it is difficult to be confident that the full range of activities are being offered and that needs are being met, and you risk the activity programme becoming a time-filler rather than an effective therapeutic tool. Equally, without planning, it is possible that residents will request an activity that has not been prepared for, or for which the equipment is not available. Yet a rigid structure can mean that opportunities are missed.

The suggested approach is one of planned flexibility. Start with a plan and be prepared to change it as necessary, so that if a group of residents decides that Bingo is not the activity of choice on a particular day – even though it may be on the programme – then the plan can be dropped and Bingo replaced with an alternative.

Having decided to pull together a plan, the first consideration is what activities to include. As previously mentioned, the guiding factors must be the needs, wishes and desires of the residents. The second consideration is the availability of resources – the residents may desire an entertainment session per week, but this may not be affordable. Resources will include the activity organiser's time; the budget; equipment and materials; the local support system, and available space. The third consideration is the other activities taking place in the home, which will guide the timings, session lengths and venues available. There is little point in planning a baking session in the morning if the products cannot be baked in the oven until late in the afternoon because of the kitchen schedule for producing meals. Equally, there is little point in booking an entertainer for a morning session if the majority of residents will still be undertaking personal care activities.

Whatever activities are planned into a programme, there must be a consideration of resident choice. Without choice and involvement, there is a strong likelihood that residents will decline to participate in the programme of activities. To promote choice, residents and relatives need to be involved: arrange discussion times; make use of Resident and Relatives meetings; talk about available activities; encourage involvement in the planning process, and advertise the programme.

When planning a programme of activity, be sensitive to age, class, culture, and background, and provide suitable sessions accordingly. Activity must be adult-orientated – this can be difficult, particularly when abilities are diminished, but many companies now provide equipment aimed at limited ability while retaining respect for the individual as an adult.

So what activities to include? A sample programme is given in Appendix 9, and Part 2 of this book explores possible activities in detail. However, a simple approach is to look at the natural daily activities and expand a timetable around this. Many people would enjoy a coffee with a friend; a walk to the park; a trip to the pub or local garden centre; tending the garden; doing some baking; tending the plants in the home, or a sherry before lunch.

Involvement of others

One of the biggest challenges facing most activity organisers is that of involving others within the activity programme. Later on, this chapter explores community groups and possible contacts for involving outsiders in the care home community, to input to the programme; but what of other staff?

It is the unfortunate experience of many activity organisers that they are often left to provide activities single-handedly; that other staff do not see the provision of activities as part of their role, or do not see how they can have the time to support the activity programme. However, there are care facilities that have successfully incorporated all staff in the provision of activities, so there follow some thoughts and practical tips and ideas on how to achieve that desired collaboration.

At the outset, the role of the senior home staff must be acknowledged. The homeowner, manager and senior care staff (qualified and unqualified) set the culture of the home. The truly successful, effective activity programme will be inextricably linked into the culture of care of the home. Without the support of the senior home team, the activity organiser will often feel isolated and separate from the rest of the care provision, and the activity programme will be something that other staff tolerate rather than truly welcome.

However, assuming that the senior staff team is supportive of activities, how do activity organisers turn that strategic support into practical support from other staff? As always, communication is the key. Wherever possible, ensure that staff are aware of the benefits of activity; what is available to residents, and what the issues and difficulties might be. There are a number of ways of doing this. As new staff (of any discipline and grade) start their employment, try to arrange time with them as part of their induction programme, or within their first few days. This is the ideal opportunity to lay out expectations before people become entrenched in the detail of day-to-day working. Prepare information that staff can be taken through, and that they can then take away with them, including aims and objectives, the importance of activities, and the benefits for residents. Outline for them the level of support that would be useful – and be realistic: whoever they are, they will be busy; they will have their own roles to undertake. It would be unrealistic to expect care staff to be able to attend and support an activity session for its full length. It would be better to ask them to make a note of what activities are on offer on the days they are on duty, and to pass on that information to residents. Explain about the need for motivating residents to attend activity sessions, and highlight the world of difference between positive motivation and asking a question – for example, 'Would you like to join the activity session – I'm sure you'd enjoy being with the others, and they serve tea during the session.' versus 'You don't want to go to Bingo, do you?'

Ask them to think through the movement of residents. Careful consideration can help to avoid and reduce unnecessary moving and handling. For example, after lunch – unless a resident specifically requests otherwise – bringing them along to the activity area rather than taking them back to their room will reduce time gathering residents for the session, as well as ensuring that they are not weary before they start, due to the effort of being transferred from armchair to wheelchair to armchair.

Encourage the staff to feel free to pop into activities, even if it is only for a couple of minutes. Residents often enjoy input from others, but make sure that staff are aware of the need to work alongside residents, rather than taking over. For example, if during a Bingo session staff are able to pop in, encourage them to help the residents keep a track of and search for the numbers on their cards, rather than doing it for them.

Ask staff to be aware that during an activity session, it is both difficult and inappropriate for the activity organiser to be tending to the personal care needs of the residents attending the session. While out of the room, attention will be diverted, concentration lost, and enjoyment of the group activity disrupted. It will be necessary for staff to assist in personal care needs during the session.

This level of support is realistic, and will go a long way towards solving some of the common issues that activity organisers raise, such as keeping residents informed, gathering groups of people together for sessions, and having residents' personal needs attended to quickly but discreetly.

Ensuring that existing staff remain aware of the benefits of activity and the levels of support needed for successful implementation is equally important: attending staff meetings and heads of department meetings will provide opportunities to keep that information fresh in the minds of other staff. Tap into in-house training programmes – particularly when care staff are undertaking N/SVQs. There are often activity-based units that the staff could complete by working alongside the activity organiser, obtaining an 'insiders view' of what it is like to plan and provide an activity session.

Use existing communication systems to inform of planned activities – the unit noticeboard; the work diary kept in the nurses' station; the communication book, for example. Detail the activities on offer: the venue; the timings, and – where possible – the names of residents who usually like to attend. This will enable staff to focus their attentions on assisting residents who like to attend specific activities, in time for them to be able to do so.

Finally, remember that staff are more likely to involve themselves in activities that they enjoy. Compile a quick tick list of activities that the residents would like and that are on offer, and ask staff to highlight the kind of activities that they themselves enjoy. Then try to include them in the provision of activities that interest them.

Resources

Very few activity organisers would describe themselves as rich in resources, so here are a few hints and tips on who to contact to access a range of different resources. There is also a list of useful telephone numbers in Appendix 2. These are national numbers, however, on enquiry they will often provide a more local contact where one is available.

Equipment

The common concerns regarding equipment are cost, ensuring age appropriateness, and quality. Fortunately, there are an increasing number of suppliers of specialist leisure equipment designed specifically for the older person. Obtaining their catalogues provides activity ideas as much as a resource for the supply of equipment. Many of the items advertised in catalogues can easily be made with a little thought and creativity. For example, floor targets comprising of old sheets with circles painted on them will work well; beanbags are easy to make, and can be constructed out of different fabrics for an enhanced sensory experience. Access to a 'handy' person who is good with wood and a jigsaw will mean that even the more complicated games, such as floor horse racing, can be made.

Alternatively, keep an eye open when visiting stores such as Pound Stretcher, Netto, and Aldi. They often sell perfectly acceptable equipment and materials at a much reduced cost.

Reminiscence materials

It is possible to purchase equipment for reminiscence, but there are materials that can trigger memories all around – photographs, objects, poetry, music, letters. Ask relatives, friends and visitors to explore their lofts for those hidden treasures. Try car boot sales – there may be items there that could be used for reminiscence.

Finally, there is no need to exclude more modern items from use in reminiscence session – for example, an electric can opener has the potential for stimulating discussions about how things have changed; what residents used to have, and what they used to use. Taking in a family wedding dress for residents to look at and handle will generate memories of their own wedding days and what was worn, as well as discussion about the availability of different fabrics, the intricacies of dressmaking, and perhaps even experiences of being a seamstress.

Entertainers

Good entertainers can be difficult to find, particularly affordable ones, so here are a few suggestions for alternatives. Try contacting:

- Local churches – their choirs may come and sing.
- The local Salvation Army band – they may come and play.
- The local school. If they are planning a play or concert, ask them if they would hold a performance in the home, or if residents could have some seats at the show.

- Local amateur dramatic groups, choral societies, etc, and ask the same.
- Local theatres – they quite often have low-cost or no-cost seats at dress rehearsals or matinee performances.
- The staff group – there might be hidden talent within the home itself.

Speakers and demonstrators

Many residents will decline the opportunity to take part in activities, but love to watch and listen. As an alternative to musical entertainers, try speakers or demonstrators. Some possible sources of speakers are

- Local Women's Institute (WI)
- Local colleges (part-time students like to show off new skills)
- Local groups – archaeological society; historical society; photographic club; railway enthusiasts.

Many residents will like to have the opportunity just to chat, and some may have limited contact with families and friends. A supply of volunteers to visit and befriend residents can be difficult to come by; however, based on the background and interests of the residents, try to link into these groups for possible visitors:

- SSAFA – Soldiers, Sailors, Air Force Association for ex-servicemen and women
- British Legion – as above
- WI; Lions Club; Round Table – good for supporting and visiting residents who were active in these groups
- Sports clubs – good for the life-time supporter
- Youth groups and schools – often as part of 'badges' or work experience.

As a final note on resources, an effective, innovative, lateral-thinking activity organiser is the best activity resource that any home can have. They have the ability to make something out of nothing; to persuade anyone and everyone to take part, and the professional cheek to beg or borrow the rest!

Advertising the planned programme

Planned programmes must be advertised, to ensure that residents, relatives and staff know what is on offer, and can make an active choice as to whether to participate. Some points to take into consideration are the following:

- Advertising the programme also advertises the service provided by the activity organiser. Ensure it is accurate, timely and professionally presented.
- Advertising a programme raises expectation – ensure that what is advertised is on offer, and provide the activity as planned. If the activity is changed, advertise this as well.

- Ensure that the programme for the forthcoming week is in place on the Friday before – then relatives visiting over the weekend will be informed and may make an active attempt to join in.
- Ensure that the programme is legible – preferably produced on a computer – and then placed where people can see it.
- Do not forget to advertise the larger events too. If there is an organised entertainer or a party, let people know.

A number of methods of advertising may be required. Consider who the advert is aimed at. Residents are unlikely to see programmes placed on a noticeboard in an entrance, whereas this would be quite appropriate for relatives and staff. A daily 'menu' – perhaps placed on a breakfast tray in the morning, or on the tables at lunchtime – or a weekly plan included on a noticeboard, in resident information booklets, or in a newsletter would be a more appropriate method of informing residents. Personal invitations to residents and relatives are also extremely effective.

Chapter 4 — Meeting the Needs of Different Client Groups

Much of the earlier chapters and the activities in Part 2 of this book refer to activities for older people with nursing and physical care needs, and occasionally for older people with dementia. This chapter looks at the needs of different client groups including older men, older people with dementia (in more detail), and younger people. It aims to explore how and why their needs differ, and then to identify the activities that can work well for each specific group. It is important to note that within every group of people there are a number of individuals, and that, as always, suggestions for specific client groups must be taken in the light of your knowledge of the individuals within the defined client group.

The activity needs of older men

It is the author's experience that many activity organisers find it difficult to identify appropriate activities for male residents. This is likely to be due in part to the fact that there are fewer men than women living in residential settings, and in part to the background experiences of men who are now in their 70s, 80s and 90s.

Fewer men within the resident group will mean fewer common interests and fewer social relationships. This leads to challenges in bringing together a group of like-minded individuals, and can lead to an increased likelihood of the men choosing to isolate themselves from the activity programme. This is not to suggest that male and female residents cannot share similar interests, or that all male residents decline to participate in activities.

Some men are subconsciously excluded from activities by staff who make assumptions and decide beforehand not to invite them along to an activity, because of a mistaken belief that they would not be interested.

The second reason that providing effective activities for men can be difficult may be related to their individual life experiences. Many men who are now in their 70s or older have had very little social time; very few leisure interests, and few hobbies. Their day is likely to have centred around employment and providing for a family. Where they did have activities, hobbies and interests outside work, they were often activities undertaken on an individual basis – for example, tending an allotment or the garden; doing work around the home, or perhaps doing woodwork, or engineering in a workshop at the end of the garden.

Not wanting to generalise means recognising that some older men may well have had a strong social circle. For example, their social group may have been getting together at the local pub or club on a regular basis, or they may have been a member of the Freemasons, the Lions Club, the British Legion or the Rotary Club. They may have been ticket-holders and regular supporters of a favourite sport or club. Equally, their only socialising may have been at work, with colleagues, or through extended families. These very specific circumstances are often difficult for a care home to recreate.

Understanding some of the reasons behind the difficulties in involving men in activities may lead to possible solutions. As with all residents, a thorough assessment and discussion of likes and dislikes, hobbies and interests will be essential to identify the areas around which activities can be developed. However, some of the following activities may be successful:

■ *Men's club:* Even if there are only a small number of men living in the care home, having a regular men's club may enable relationships to develop and more activity interests to be triggered. The frequency of such a group will depend solely on the needs of the individuals within the group and may be weekly, fortnightly or monthly. The group should meet for a specific purpose, whether a general discussion or a shared activity. Wherever possible, the men's club should be organised and facilitated by a man – perhaps a more able resident, a staff member, a volunteer, or a family member.

■ *Sport-based activities:* Plan an activity session around a sporting fixture, either shown on television or after the event, on video. Cricket tests, Wimbledon, horse-racing, motor-racing, football and rugby matches would all lend themselves to activity sessions. Where possible, be familiar with specific sporting interests and clubs supported, to ensure interest and relevance. Be aware that this kind of activity is often enjoyed by the ladies, and may provide an opportunity for the men to develop social relationships with all of their peers, not just the other men!

■ *Work-type activities:* As mentioned above, work-based sessions are generally popular, and the male residents may enjoy taking on specific roles, or undertaking this kind of activity. Again, avoid making assumptions about the work-type occupations that could be made available to the men. They may enjoy the opportunity to work in the garden, or tend the plants in the home; however, they may also respond positively to some of the more domestic pursuits, particularly if these have featured in their role within their family.

■ *Creative activities:* If the resident has enjoyed creative hobbies in the past such as carpentry, gardening or painting, these may be activities that can be developed further. Many craft resources provide wood kits for varying ability levels, from requiring the skill to use a full range of tools to simply completing a project through staining and varnishing.

■ *Alcohol-based sessions:* If the common social experience of the group was based around attending the local pub or club, try a trip out for a pint or a pub lunch, or perhaps bring the pub into the home. Try a beer-tasting session, or have preferred drinks available as an alternative to the usual tea and coffee refreshments, supported by an afternoon of pub games such as darts, dominoes, cards, pool and billiards.

The activity needs of people with dementia

The importance of assessing and identifying the interests and needs of residents is never more important than with people with dementia, for they may have difficulty in verbalising their likes and dislikes. Identifying the activity needs of people with dementia requires knowledge and information from a number of sources. Knowledge on the part of the activity organiser of dementia, the dementia process, and the effect that this may have on the individual. Knowledge of the individual themselves, their behaviours, their communications (verbal and non-verbal), and their responses to different situations and scenarios; and most importantly, knowledge of the individual's background: their previous likes and dislikes; their values and beliefs.

This information can be brought together to identify the activities that the individual may enjoy (many of which are described in Part 2), and the approach that the organiser needs to take.

The manner in which the activity should be offered, and the way in which the individual should be involved, will reflect the skills and abilities of the person with dementia:

- Concentration and attention span is likely to be limited, therefore activities should be kept straightforward and short.
- Instructions from the activity organiser should be kept simple, introducing a 'task' at a time and allowing that element to be completed before giving any further instruction.
- Complete flexibility is required on the part of the activity organiser, to respond to fluctuations in interest and ability level of the individual and the group.
- The activity should allow for residents to come and go; for partnership working and for spontaneous development as the residents may decide to take the activity off in a different direction.

As previously mentioned, many of the activities described in Part 2 will be appropriate for people with dementia. A number of other activities will be particularly effective:

- *Sensory sessions:* People with dementia can often be engaged and stimulated through use of the senses. Multi-sensory environments are becoming more popular in dementia care facilities, as more anecdotal and research-based evidence becomes available.

- *Work-type occupation:* This kind of session – particularly domestic-chore-type activities, including cooking and gardening, are often very successful due to their familiarity – the fact that the skills are often well rehearsed and held almost subconsciously – the opportunity for subtle role modelling, and the low importance of an outcome.

■ *Musical events:* An effective kind of activity for all resident groups. Whether listening to music, dancing, singing, or playing instruments, many activity organisers have reported particular success with this kind of session with people with dementia.

■ *Physical movement:* Many people with dementia stay physically able for longer, and show behaviours that seem to indicate a need for exercise and movement. Care should be taken that the activity is adapted to the appropriate level for the group. Some residents with dementia need to have a purpose for a session, and throwing a ball from person to person may not offer that purpose, whereas involvement in a target game with a score and a winner may do so.

The activity needs of younger residents

More and more care homes are beginning to explore the provision of services for alternative client groups, in particular younger people with physical disabilities, learning disabilities, traumatic injuries, or neurological conditions. As with all individuals, these younger clients have a need for effective group and individual activities, although their needs may be very different – including the focus of their care.

Younger people are more likely to move into a care home for respite – for short periods of a week to a month to provide a break; or for rehabilitation, with the long-term aim of moving on from the care home, possibly back home or to another long-term, continuing care facility. The nature of their stay will affect the approach to activities and the kind of activities to be offered.

Clients who move into a care home for respite may not be well known to the activity organiser. Some will stay for respite on a regular basis and, over time, will become known. But finding out their likes and dislikes may be more difficult. The respite resident coming in for a break may wish to do just that – have a break from everything – and may wish to have very little involvement in the activity programme. For others, the move into the care home may offer the supportive environment needed to enable them to function more fully, and to be actively involved in all activities. This should be established as soon as possible, so the activity organiser can tailor the involvement accordingly.

Clients who move into a care home for rehabilitation will expect exactly that – activities that enable skill development and improvement towards an agreed aim. To provide this kind of activity, guidance is required from a multi-professional team including physiotherapists, occupational therapists and speech and language therapists. These professionals will complete a full assessment of ability, and then devise a programme of treatment and activity that will move the individual towards their goal. Under these circumstances, some of the activities required will be of a treatment nature, others will be more social.

In an ideal setting, younger people will be cared for within specialist units, among other residents of a similar age, and with a similar disability or condition. However, it is not unusual for homes to take younger people – generally in very small numbers – into the main care home with older people. This will obviously generate a different range of group dynamics. There may be many activities that younger and older people can enjoy together; but there is also likely to be a need for activities aimed at the younger people – probably offered on a more individual basis.

The following suggestions are for activity-types that may be especially effective with younger people:

■ *Community contact:* Particularly important for residents admitted for respite, and who are hoping to move back into the community, to maintain and develop contacts and access to resources that are or will be of use. This will include researching local resources; making contacts; arranging for visitors to come to the home; and arranging outings from the home. Useful contacts will include daycare facilities, clubs and organisations, transport resources, and volunteer groups.

■ *Physical movement:* Involvement in this type of activity should be under the guidance of the physiotherapist, when offered as part of rehabilitation, to ensure that the activity is offered at the correct level. The aim should be to offer a challenge without over stretching the individual, and to highlight areas to focus on – for example, working on balance, upper limb movement, or upper limb strength.

■ *Domestic-type sessions:* Again, particularly important for those undergoing rehabilitation, this kind of activity should be provided under the guidance of an occupational therapist, who will advise on adapted equipment that may be required and problem-solving approaches to everyday tasks. The aim should be to develop the skills necessary for the individual to undertake the particular tasks on their return home.

■ *Creative activities:* Particularly useful for upper limb work, to develop grip and range of movement, but also useful as a communication tool, although guidance may be needed from an art, music or drama therapist.

Chapter 5 Evaluation and Documentation

Evaluation

Providing an effective group activity programme is not a static process: the activities on offer should reflect the needs and wishes of the resident group, and the resident group will change. New residents will move into the home, with different abilities and interests, existing residents' needs will change as their abilities change, and as time goes by.

In order to ensure that your activity programme stays in touch with the resident group, regular evaluation is necessary. There are a number of ways of evaluating the programme:

- Resident feedback
- Staff feedback
- Relatives feedback
- Review of documentation.

Resident feedback can be obtained both formally and informally. During day-to-day activity, feedback can be requested – for example, 'Did you enjoy the quiz yesterday?'; 'I haven't seen you at many activities recently, is there anything you would like to do?' More formally, questionnaires (such as the sample in Appendix 3) distributed on a regular basis, asking residents to comment on the range of activities on offer, and inviting suggestions for alternative activities, can be useful, although consideration should be given to the abilities of the resident group to fill in the questionnaire. If assisted in its completion, particularly by the activity organiser, residents may not feel comfortable in being seen to 'criticise' the current activities. Residents' meetings can be used to open up discussions about the activity programme, which can provide the opportunity for comments on existing activities and ideas for future activities.

Staff feedback can also be gathered formally and informally. Staff may well pass on comments on behalf of the residents, particularly if they are made aware that the feedback would be welcome. For example, as they are offering personal care, residents may tell them how much they enjoyed a particular entertainer or outing and staff can then pass this on. More formal feedback can be gathered through attending staff meetings to discuss the activities on offer and ideas for future activities. Often, involving staff in this kind of discussion can also identify resources – staff with particular activity interests may be willing to be involved further in future activities. Feedback from relatives can be gathered in similar ways – through discussion on a daily basis, through open invitation to share any feedback passed to them by residents, and through relatives' meetings.

The activity organiser should get a sense of the effectiveness of the activity programme through the attendance and participation levels of residents. If residents are not coming along to activities, or alternatively if a room is consistently full, then this gives some indication as to how much the residents are enjoying that particular activity. On occasion, however, it may be useful to review the activity-based documentation.

Documentation

Many activity organisers find it difficult to justify spending time on documentation and record-keeping, preferring to spend as much time as possible with the residents providing group activities. While this is an admirable position, without effective documentation activity organisers and other staff will find it difficult to accurately review the standards of activity provision. Should the activity personnel change, then documentation provides information for new staff, enabling a smoother transition from one activity organiser to another. As the health and social care authorities become more interested in effective activities, then there will be an increased demand to see the 'evidence' of residents' involvement in activities. It is also the author's opinion that without documentation, activities will continue to be an add-on, an extra – something that residents can do without. The giving of treatment – medication, changing a dressing, or providing a bath – is always documented. Activities should be too.

The compromise, therefore, is to have a documentation system that is useful in terms of the information it records, yet not onerous in the time and effort required to complete it. With this in mind, there are four kinds of information that will be useful:

1 Background information regarding the residents' experiences, likes, dislikes, needs and abilities
2 Information regarding the range of activities offered
3 Information of a quantitative nature regarding the attendance of residents at activities
4 Information of a qualitative nature regarding the benefits of attending activities.

The background information should be a document that can be added to by all – residents and relatives as well as staff. It should be remembered that this is a confidential document, and should be treated with respect. This document is likely to be dynamic, with additional information included as it becomes known. Information that would be useful to collect would be previous hobbies and interests; previous occupations; life history, in terms of places lived, schooling and family, as well as an indication as to the kind of activities in which the resident might like to be involved. This should be supported by information about their health and abilities, including mobility levels; cognitive abilities such as concentration and memory; communication abilities; sensory abilities regarding sight and hearing, and health considerations of use to the activity organiser, such as the presence of diabetes or epilepsy. (A sample form is available in Appendix 1.)

The information regarding the activities on offer will often take the form of the programme. Keeping back-copies of the activity programme provides an ever-growing resource of activity ideas, as well as evidence of the range of activities that have been offered. New staff can see easily what activities have been offered on both a regular basis and over time.

The quantitative data and the qualitative data can be combined into one format, although this may make completion more time-consuming. Documenting on a daily basis what the resident has participated in, and any feedback or response, can also lead to repetitive information, which has little use or value. More appropriate is a daily 'numbers' record of who has attended the activities on offer, supported by a qualitative summary of the residents' responses and feedback on a less regular basis – perhaps weekly or monthly, as suits the care home.

The numbers record can be in the form of a diary, by simply listing the names of residents who attended the activities of the day. Alternatively, this could take the form of a tick sheet, whereby the activity offered and the date is written at the top of a column, and ticks are placed alongside the names of those who have attended. It may be useful to include on this kind of form when a resident declines the opportunity to attend, or when an external factor has meant that they have been unable to attend – for example, if they had a visitor or were unwell. When this document is evaluated it will then be easier to gather a fuller picture of the popular activities, and also to identify the residents who are not attending activities, but who may benefit from individual type activities. (A sample form is in Appendix 4.)

The qualitative statement can be compiled on a progress notes page. The entry should be dated. It should include a summary for the week or month of the activities attended; the levels of enjoyment and participation observed, and any responses of interest – for example, information shared during a reminiscence session that had not been shared before. Each entry should be signed, as the statement will form part of the resident's legal care records. (A sample form is in Appendix 8.)

It must be remembered that all documentation about a resident forms part of their overall care record, and as such may be viewed, under agreed arrangements, by the resident themselves, their family or visiting professionals.

Part 2

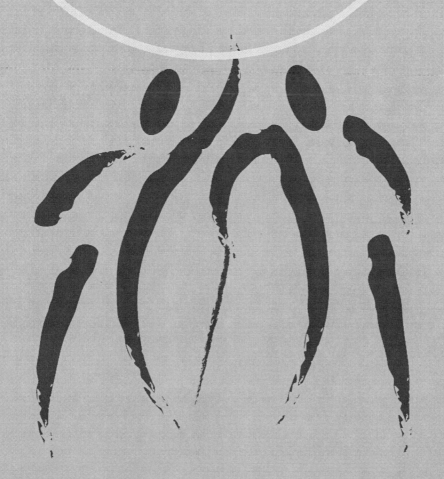

Chapter 6 The Ten Areas of Need Approach

What activities to do

One of the biggest concerns facing activity organisers is what activities to do – being able to come up with new ideas that residents are going to want to participate in and enjoy. Earlier chapters explored the difference between filling time and meeting needs; the need for assessment to identify the skills and difficulties of the resident group; and the overall desire to provide activities that are failure-free, as well as offering the required challenge. Resting on a background assumption that the activities offered should be resident-centred, based on the likes and dislikes of the resident group, this chapter looks more specifically at what activities to do, and the information needed to pick up on some of the ideas and make them happen.

The 10 areas of need approach

It is important to define what is meant by 'need'. The dictionary defines need as 'that which is required or desired'. Activities that are desired are those in which residents express an interest – a desire to undertake. What about 'that which is required' – the activities that residents need? Their physical wellbeing may require attention: they may be physically unwell; they may be physically unfit; they may behave in a way, that indicates they require physically based activities – for example, moving furniture or constantly walking around. But humans are more than physical beings – there are a number of other human needs, which can be combined together to give 10 areas of activity need:

1 *Physical needs:* To encourage movement; to encourage exercise; to retain levels of physical ability; to reduce stiffness; to promote circulation.

2 *Intellectual needs:* To facilitate cognitive stimulation; to keep the mind active; the brain ticking.

3 *Creative needs:* To provide an opportunity for self-expression; to promote creativity; to facilitate giving.

4 *Social needs:* To promote social engagement, spending time with others, developing friendships and meaningful relationships.

5 *Sensory needs:* To maintain sensory awareness and ability; to encourage communication and self-expression.

6 *Self esteem needs:* To promote a sense of self-worth, a sense of value, a sense of importance, a sense of feeling cared for and caring for.

7 *Spiritual needs:* To address spirituality and religious beliefs.

8 *Cultural needs:* To address cultural interests; to retain contact with local cultures and customs; to retain personal identities.

9 *Emotional needs:* To address the emotional aspects of the individual; to facilitate a sense of wellbeing; to encourage communication and satisfaction.

10 *Educational and Employment needs:* To facilitate continued learning and development; to encourage role satisfaction and identity; to create a sense of value and purposefulness.

If activities can be included from each of the 10 areas of need within the activity programme, then many of the residents' needs will be met. That is not to suggest that activities from each of the 10 areas should be provided every day, every week or every month. The frequency with which the type of activity is offered will be based on the resident group, and on how often they desire that type of activity. The specific activity that is provided within the 10 areas of need will be dictated by the resident group, based on their likes and dislikes.

Putting the 10 areas of need into practice

Appendix 5 contains a checklist of ideas and suggestions for activities that could fall within each of the 10 areas of need. Some activities appear under a number of headings as they address a variety of different needs. For example, a party should have a strong social element, but may involve physical and cognitive activities, and may also have a sensory component. For ease of reference, activities are included under one area of need when it is clear that is the primary focus of the activity, and under a number of areas of need when the approach to the activity may affect the demands that it makes.

The rest of this chapter explores in more detail the rationale behind the areas of need, and provides the information required to implement those activities.

Depending upon the client group, the residents' abilities will vary from physically very able to physically very disabled. It is important that, whatever level of ability is present, the activities provided enable residents, as a minimum, to retain that level of ability. The old adage holds true – 'use it or lose it'. It is often difficult to retain physical abilities, particularly in environments where importance is placed on undertaking tasks as quickly as possible. In this kind of environment, it is not unusual for staff to transport residents to and from communal areas in wheelchairs, even when they are capable of walking the distance required, albeit slowly. This makes residents more reliant on the activity programme to meet their physical activity needs.

People with dementia can remain quite physically able, often with fairly high energy levels, resulting in reasonably high levels of physical activity. Focusing that energy into physically based activities may address some of the unsettled behaviour, as well as providing the opportunity to retain mobility, strength and stability.

It is worth noting that physical exercise does not have to be offered only in the traditional format. Much can be gained through physically based games; however, the wishes and expectations of the resident group should be paramount in choosing the direction to take. Some residents will not wish to participate in 'formal' exercise sessions, such as armchair exercises or movement to music. Others will not wish to participate in childlike games, such as target activities and skittles.

Activity **Traditional Exercises**

Benefits: **Good all round exercise session, works upper and lower limbs, improving or maintaining range of movement, balance and coordination, as well as being fun.**

Equipment: Exercise routine (Speechmark and Winslow/Rompa supply exercise routines – see Appendix 2 for contact details). Appropriate music (if desired by resident group); balls; beanbags, scarves.

Duration: 20–30 minutes. Can be extended by finishing session listening to music, with a drink.

Procedure: Ensure that everyone can see and hear. Introduce each exercise describing and demonstrating clearly what they should do. Include movements such as shrugging shoulders, lifting arms, clapping, seated marching, straightening and lifting legs, pointing toes. Take each movement slowly, helping residents as required. Include activities with equipment such as balls and scarves if residents are interested. Include a warm-up and cool-down at the beginning and end by making the movements slower, keeping the arms down and taking some deep breaths.

Hints: If there are concerns about leading an exercise session, speak to a physiotherapist or exercise therapist to see if they might assist. Strength or resistance exercises should not be undertaken by anyone unless they are qualified to do so.

Some residents will want their exercise session to be taken seriously, as a therapy session, others will want to have fun using music, balls, scarves – be sure about the desires of the resident group.

Speechmark

Activity **Balloon Handball**

Benefits: **Helps with coordination, general exercise, upper limb movement and balance, as well as encouraging a sense of achievement and lots of fun. Ideal for those concerned about being hit by a ball, although be aware of residents who do not like balloons.**

Equipment: Large balloons, music.

Procedure: Arrange the room so residents are able to sit in a circle, close enough to others so that the balloon can reach them.

Put on the music and encourage residents to move the balloon backwards and forwards to the group leader, or to other residents, by use of hand, head or foot, or by any means – whichever is comfortable and acceptable to them.

Alternatives: Provide a net across which the balloon can be tapped, as in tennis.

Try taking a team approach, grouping residents together to develop a level of competition.

Hints: Try to ensure that stray balloons do not accidentally involve residents who do not wish to participate, but who may be in the same area as the activity.

It is possible to purchase (from Rompa and others – see Appendix 2) lightweight balls for this activity that have additional sensory features, such as bells, rice, or objects. They may be scented and textured to increase the benefits of the activity and enable those with sensory impairment to participate.

Speechmark

Activity | **Target Game**

Benefits: **Improves hand–eye coordination; upper limb movement; upper limb strength; concentration, and attention span. If a resident is able to undertake the activity standing, then it will also be good for balance and stability. The activity can be used to encourage number skills, by encouraging residents to count and add up their scores.**

Equipment: Floor targets with beanbags (easy to make). Floor netball sets (ball and a low-level laundry basket would do just as well). Scoreboard.

Procedure: Set up the games at a reasonable length away from each resident in turn. Ask and encourage the resident to throw the beanbag on to the floor target, or the ball into the basket. Encourage scoring where competition is acceptable to the group.

Hints: This is a one-to-one activity centred within a group; individuals take turns, while other residents look on. Residents with limited attention span may become disinterested if the group is too large and it takes too long for their turn to come around.

To make the floor target, use an old sheet or piece of plastic. Paint on circles, either separately in different areas of the mat, or within each other: start with a small circle, paint a larger circle around it and a larger one around that, and so on. Give each circle a number – for example 5, 10, 15, 20, 25, 50, corresponding to the level of skill required to land the beanbag in the circle – this will be the score that the individual gets if their beanbag lands in that circle.

Speechmark

Activity **Parachute Game**

Benefits: **Good exercise and great for coordination, balance and upper limb movement. Can help to build relationships between individual residents, and residents and staff.**

Equipment: Parachute (obtained from Rompa – see Appendix 2) or lightweight material of a similar size (see below). Music, balls, space.

Procedure: Try to encourage the residents to either all stand or all sit down, as it makes things easier. Ask them to hold an edge of the parachute and gently wave it up and down. This can be done to music. Telling the residents to be gentle, fast, slow or brisk not only encourages play, but also enables an assessment of awareness of instructions. This game can be lots of fun for both residents and carers.

Alternatives: Increase the difficulty by placing a ball or balloon in the centre of the parachute and encouraging everyone to keep it on the parachute.

Hints: Be aware that people can tire easily with this activity, and some may become quite aggressive. This activity should not be continued for too long, due to the excessive movement placed through the wrists and arms that can cause discomfort.

Parachutes may be quite expensive to purchase; however lightweight fabric can be equally effective, especially silk-based fabric. Bright colours will increase the sensory effect. Strips of fabric in different colours can be sewn together to make the parachute. The size will depend on the number of people likely to join in. Ensure that there is a solid edge to grip and preferably handles for people to hold.

Activity Skittles and Carpet Bowls

Benefits: **Good for upper limb movement, hand–eye coordination, upper limb strength, number skills.**

Equipment: Skittle set, or carpet bowls set. Scoreboard.

Procedure: Invite residents to roll the ball at the skittles or jack (small target ball in bowls), which should be placed in front of each resident in turn at such a distance as to enable success. Encourage residents to work out and remember their score (but keep a separate record). Decide beforehand how many throws each resident can have on each occasion, and how many rounds to have; or aim for a certain score.

Alternatives: Try forming members into groups and generate team scores rather than individual scores. This can be an ongoing activity with weekly winners advertised on noticeboards; or a cup for the monthly winner or winning team.

Hints: Make sure that the skittles used are sturdy enough to stand but light enough to be knocked down easily, to ensure success for those with limited upper limb strength. Be aware of stray balls, particularly if they are aimed with any force. For residents with visual impairment, use brightly coloured skittles and bowls and the group leader's voice as a guide for them to aim towards. Depending upon the size of the ball, an open plastic drainpipe can be used to roll the ball down towards the skittle or jack. This will be particularly useful for those with limited upper body movement.

Group Activities with Older Adults © Vicki Dent 2003

Activity **Darts**

Benefits: **Good for upper limb movement, hand–eye coordination, upper limb strength, concentration, and number skills. If able to stand, will also aid balance and stability.**

Equipment: Magnetic or safety dart board and darts. Table. Scoreboard.

Procedure: Invite residents to throw darts in turn at the dart board. Encourage them to work out and remember their score (but keep a separate record). Decide beforehand how many throws each resident can have on each occasion, and how many rounds to have; or aim for the first person to reach a certain score.

Alternatives: Think about keeping a running score total, and have a weekly or monthly champion. This activity is also appropriate as a team game.

Hints: Safety darts boards are usually table-top in style, so putting the board on to a bed table will let you move the board in front of each resident.

This activity could also be taken to people in their rooms, if they wish to participate but are reluctant to come along to the communal area. Their scores can be kept alongside those of the individuals playing in the lounge, and this might generate enough interest for them to come along to see the people they are beating, or who are beating them!

This activity is particularly successful with men, but should obviously not be aimed at men alone.

Speechmark

Activity **Yoga**

Benefits: **Good all-round exercise session, works upper and lower limbs, improving or maintaining range of movement, balance and coordination, as well as being fun and relaxing.**

Equipment: This kind of session is best taught by a qualified yoga teacher. Local instructors can be identified through adult education organisations, or through the national organisation (see Appendix 2).

Procedure: Each yoga teacher will wish to run their sessions in their own way. Before offering yoga to the residents, spend time with the instructor ensuring that they are aware of the abilities and limitations of both the participating group and the environment. An adapted yoga session focusing on breathing and gentle stretching to encourage relaxation is likely to be of the most interest and benefit to the resident group.

Hints: Many residents may not have had the opportunity to partake in yoga previously. Any arrangement with an external session leader should be made on a trial basis to 'test the water', to see if residents both attend and enjoy the session offered, before entering into a long-term arrangement.

Speechmark

Activity Outdoor Activities

Benefits: **Provide general exercise combined with the benefits of fresh air and sensory stimulation offered by being outside.**

Equipment: Dependant on the activity.

Ideas: Walking in the garden, lawn croquet, golf putting green.

Procedure: Ensure that everyone participating in activities outdoors is appropriately protected from the weather with sun screen, sun hats, sensible footwear, coats, hats and scarves as required. Ensure that refreshments are handy if the weather is pleasant, to avoid any risk of dehydration. Outdoor activities should be undertaken on level ground, as even those quite able to stand may find the external environment more unsteady.

- Garden walk – excellent general exercise, can include those who are unable to walk by use of a wheelchair. Activity can be enhanced through general discussion and sensory activity – looking at and smelling flowers growing in the garden.

- Lawn croquet – lawn sets can be purchased from sports shops or through suppliers such as Rompa and Nottingham Rehab. (See Appendix 2.) Individuals take turns to work their way around a croquet course, knocking their ball through hoops fixed into the ground using croquet mallets.

- Golf putting – small holes can be made in the grass, large enough to take a small flowerpot, to act as the golf hole. Then residents can practise their putting from a distance that they choose. This can also be undertaken sitting down.

Speechmark

As with physical skills, the more that individuals make use of their cognitive skills, the more alert and aware they will remain – including people with cognitive impairment (through dementia or brain injury). The key is having an understanding of the resident group, their likes and dislikes, and their ability levels. Most cognitive-based activities can be graded to suit a range of abilities; however, consideration should be given to the ability levels of the individuals to be included in a group. If the ability range is too diverse, then some members of the group will be frustrated: the activities will be either too easy or too hard. It may be necessary to consider offering a particular activity twice, aimed at different ability levels.

Quick tip: discuss the level of the session with staff beforehand, so that they are aware of which residents could be invited to the session. This will avoid the scenario of residents who might find the level too easy or too difficult being brought to a session by another staff member. For successful cognitive activities, there needs to be an overwhelming sense of achievement with an underpinning degree of challenge.

Resources for cognitive activities need not be expensive; quiz books are available from Speechmark (see Appendix 2 for contact details), and most local bookshops. Take a look in the bigger supermarkets – they often stock a range that are really good value. Newspapers and magazines always feature word games, crosswords and quizzes that can be used. Television programmes are a great source of ideas for quiz-type games. Again, know the residents, be aware of the kind of general knowledge they have and the topics that they enjoy, and develop the quizzes and games around them.

Activity | **Memory Tray (Kim's Game)**

Benefits: **Great for mental stimulation, memory, concentration, and attention span.**

Equipment: A tray, six or seven familiar objects (glass, photo-frame, spoon, pen, etc), and a cloth large enough to cover the objects on the tray.

Procedure: Place all of the objects on to the tray, and cover them with the cloth. Inform the residents that the cloth will be removed for a few minutes, and ask them to try to memorise the objects on the tray. After a couple of minutes cover the items again and ask the residents to recall the items on the tray.

Alternatives: This can be undertaken as a group or individual activity. For those with good understanding but limited verbal skills photographs of the items mixed with photographs of other objects, or a board with the items written down mixed in among other item words, could be used. The resident could then point to the items that they thought were on the tray. (Decide in advance how many attempts they could have at guessing the items, otherwise they will complete the task by a process of elimination!)

As an alternative, the residents could study the tray for a few minutes, before you take it out of sight and remove an item or items. Bring the tray back to the group and see who can identify the missing item(s).

Speechmark

Activity Newspapers and Magazines

Benefits: Mental stimulation, memory, concentration, attention, orientation, and communication.

Equipment: Daily and local papers; magazines of interest to the group.

Procedure: Sitting with either an individual or a group of residents, read through the headlines; encourage discussion about different features; concentrate on local stories (residents may know the people featured); read through horoscopes; complete the crosswords.

Alternatives: With a more able group of residents, encourage residents to present a story of their choice to the other residents, and then open up a discussion on the story.

Develop a home newspaper or newsletter. Residents could write or dictate articles and features. The group could be responsible for editing and compiling the newspaper or newsletter.

Hints: Try not to make assumptions about the stories residents may or may not be interested in. Offer the headline or a brief summary, and invite the group to choose whether they would like to hear more.

Questions may be asked about the stories featured, so try to be prepared with additional information if required.

This activity can be used as a warm-up activity before starting the main session. It is particularly useful if residents are joining the group in dribs and drabs, engaging and stimulating those present, yet not being disrupted by others joining the group.

Careful selection of the newspapers to use is needed – consider daily papers and broadsheets.

Many newspapers, magazines and books are now available on cassette tape or in large print, for those who find it difficult to read. See Appendix 2 for contact details for talking newspapers and big-print newspapers, or contact the local library for further information.

Speechmark

Activity **Word Games and Quizzes**

Benefits: **Mental stimulation, memory, concentration, attention, orientation, and communication.**

Equipment: Quiz ideas, quiz books, flipchart with pad, pens, paper; access to a photocopier.

Procedure: There are many different kinds of word games and quizzes (a small range can be found in Appendix 6), and a number of different approaches to running a quiz session:

- *Residents working individually*, writing down answers, competing against each other.

- *Residents working in teams*, with one member acting as scribe, writing down the answers.

- *Residents working together as a whole group*, with the group leader acting as scribe on a flipchart.

Ideas: Crosswords, anagram quizzes, themed quizzes (royalty, colours, food, places), word searches, alphabet games, hangman, blockbuster-based quizzes, smell quizzes, tactile quizzes (see page 74, Sensory Activities, for more detail), music quizzes.

Alternative: Residents who do not attend activities can also participate in word games and quizzes. Photocopies of the quizzes or word games can be distributed to residents in their rooms for completion at their own pace and in their own time. Alternatively, have a home quiz or crossword. Enlarge the quiz or crossword, and display it in a central place in the home; encourage all who pass it (staff, residents, families) to have a go at answering a question, or filling in an answer.

Hints: For those whose spelling is not wonderful, encourage other residents to help out.

Keep a file of all the quizzes and word games that have been used – in six months or a year the resident group is likely to have changed, and the quiz can be re-used.

Speechmark

Activity **Jigsaws**

Benefits: **Mental stimulation, memory, concentration, and attention. Good for hand–eye coordination. Requires a degree of grip strength and dexterity for manipulating the pieces.**

Equipment: Appropriate style and size jigsaw puzzles.

Procedure: This kind of activity is better run on a one-to-one basis. Sit with a resident to ensure that they are clear about the picture to be put together; then work together. This activity can be graded to suit the skills of the individual. Residents could work independently, under supervision. They could find pieces under direct instruction – 'Find a corner, find the blue sky pieces.' They could tell the group leader where to put pieces. Pieces could be selected, and the resident would then advise on where the piece should go with the resident completing the final stage of putting the piece in its rightful place. Encourage the residents to work to their optimum level.

Alternative: Have a home jigsaw. If space is available, leave a jigsaw in a central place and encourage residents, staff and families to have a go whenever they are passing.

Hints: It is possible to purchase jigsaw puzzles that are appropriate for adults, as well as having small numbers of large pieces to aid those who would have difficulty undertaking a more traditional 500- or 1000-piece puzzle.

Jigsaw puzzles are a great resource to leave around in communal areas for all to access, including families and visitors, who are often grateful for having something to do during their visits.

Speechmark

Activity **Discussions**

Benefits: **Mental stimulation, memory, concentration, attention, orientation, and communication skills. Also aids reminiscence and information-sharing – good for finding out more about residents.**

Equipment: Ideas and triggers – pictures, photos, newspaper stories, music, poetry, speakers, slide shows, themes, personal interests.

Procedure: Identify a topic of interest to the residents, then encourage discussion – either with an individual or with a small group. Be aware that running a discussion with a group requires careful management, to make sure people hear what is said and can follow the discussion to be able to contribute.

Alternatives: Invite a speaker to generate a discussion through a slide show, presentation, or demonstration of their skills, interests or role. Speakers could be residents with a particular interest, family members, or staff members. Try contacting organisations such as Age Concern, Women's Institutes, Lions Clubs, community organisations or adult education colleges for potential speakers.

Sample topics: Topics will be as varied as the contacts made, but here are a few ideas – hatmakers; holiday picture shows; countryside talks with slide shows; flower arranging demonstration; complementary therapy talks and demonstrations; health and beauty companies; pearly king and queens; wildlife sanctuaries; charitable organisations; sugar craft demonstrations; Guide Dogs for the Blind; Hearing Dogs for the Deaf; Fire Brigade; Police Force; collectors – plates, Toby jugs, teddy bears, thimbles, reminiscence materials.

Activity Table Games

Benefits: **Mental stimulation, attention, concentration, number skills. Requires a degree of dexterity to manipulate the pieces.**

Equipment: Packs of cards, board games, dominoes, and the knowledge of how to play. Large playing cards, large-print playing cards and adapted dominoes (size and colour) are all available from Nottingham Rehab and Rompa (see Appendix 2).

Procedure: The size of group for these activities should be based on the number of players needed for the game. If it is larger than that, residents will need to pair up or watch – both of which are perfectly acceptable alternatives.

Hints: Try a table games afternoon with a range of activities on offer that residents could choose from. If taking this approach, consider who will 'run' each game – without somebody taking the lead, it is not unusual for play to cease!

Whatever game is being played, check that the players are playing to the same rules, even if those rules are different from traditional rules. Who says that dominoes or a board game has to be played in a certain way? The aim is to engage, therefore be prepared to 'go with the flow'.

Some of the games that could be played may be based on children's games, and if purchased from children's shops will be bright in colour with larger pieces, and therefore easier for the residents to engage with. Store these items out of their original boxes, which are likely to have references to children on them, to avoid any risk of offence.

This page may be photocopied for instructional use only. *Group Activities with Older Adults* © Vicki Dent 2003

Speechmark

Activity | Reminiscence

Benefits: **Mental stimulation, concentration, communication, increased sense of self worth, opportunity to share, increased awareness, and knowledge of the resident.**

Equipment: Themes (see ideas below). Triggers – photographs, objects, poetry, stories, magazines.

Procedure: Reminiscence sessions can be run in a number of ways – individually or with a group; free-flowing, or focused around a theme.

For those who may have difficulty initially recalling memories, a trigger is essential – photographs, objects, a piece of music, an item of food or a piece of poetry, will all provide a focus for thought. A box of items around a theme should also provide a focus, as well as offer additional intrigue and excitement about what is in the box. For example, a box containing nappies (disposable and terry), nappy cream, talc, nappy pins, a potty, a baby bath, babycare books, and photographs of babies would be useful in developing thoughts and shared experiences around childcare.

Ideas: Childcare, schooldays, games and toys, holidays, weddings, work, household chores, wash day, transport, cooking, clothing and fashion, royal family, theatre and film stars, music and entertainers.

Alternatives: Think about what might be done with shared experiences and memories (with people's permission): develop life stories for the individuals involved. Display thoughts and stories, typed up, in a book or around the home. Create artwork or collages based on the thoughts and memories. Develop a cookbook based on shared recipes. Share thoughts and memories with local schools, museums, and interested local organisations.

Hints: Many residents appear to dislike the idea of attending a 'reminiscence session' but will happily attend a 'discussion' session and reminisce freely – it seems to be related to what the session is called!

Speechmark

Activity **Pairs Game**

Benefits: **Mental stimulation, concentration.**

Equipment: This is a game based on the card game 'pairs', whereby players have to memorise the whereabouts of different cards to select matching pairs.

Preparation: Gather together 10 pictures or photographs of meaning and relevance to the group that will play. Ensure that each picture or photograph is printed in landscape style. Enlarge each picture or photograph to A4 size. Make a second copy of each picture or photograph. Place each of the now 20 pictures or photographs into an A4 plastic punched pocket, of the type used to file papers in ringbinders. Place a piece of paper with a number on it from 1 to 20 on the reverse of the picture, inside the plastic pocket. Tie a piece of string through the centre hole on the side of the plastic pocket. Pass a safety pin through the string. Take a large sheet and then pin each plastic pocket containing a picture or photograph and a number to the sheet. Ensure that the matching pictures or photographs are not pinned next to one another. When playing, the sheet will need to be held or fixed to a wall for all to see.

Procedure: Make sure all of the pockets have the numbers facing the resident group. Place the sheet so that all playing can see clearly, and then ask a resident to choose two numbers, from 1 to 20. Turn over the pockets with the chosen numbers, so that the resident can see if the photos or pictures are the same. Ensure that all those playing have ascertained the content of the two pictures on show. If the two pictures match then the resident who selected the numbers wins a point. If not, the two pockets are turned back over and another resident makes the number selection. The aim is for the residents to remember where the photos or pictures are, and to find the matching pairs.

Hints: The photographs and pictures should be simple in style, and the content should be of familiar items or people – for example staff and residents of the home, animals, flowers, places, famous people.

This could be offered as a group or team game. As an alternative to giving points for matching pairs, time how long it takes for the group to find all of the pairs.

Speechmark

Activity | Life-History Books

Benefits: **Can help with memory, triggering reminiscence. Could aid carers' knowledge of the residents. Fun, communication, increases feelings of self worth and value.**

Equipment: Scrapbook, photograph album, photographs, and written accounts.

Duration: This is an ongoing activity. As memories are shared then the life-history book can be added to. Each session should be as long as the resident wishes it to be.

Procedure: Life-history books are a method of gaining additional information about the resident, encouraging reminiscence, adding value to memories and thoughts shared. This is an activity that can involve everyone – the activity organiser, carers and families.

Provide the residents with their own scrapbook or photograph album. As they share stories and memories, these should be written out (with the resident's permission) by the person hearing the memory, and then fixed into the life-history book. The stored records can then be enhanced with photographs, pictures, fabric – anything that enhances the information.

Hints: The life-history books should be developed over time, with additional information included as it is shared. If concentration and memory begins to deteriorate, the life-history books can be used to aid recall and, finally, the life histories can be passed to the family if they so desire.

Speechmark

Creativity offers the opportunity for self-expression; may provide an opportunity for continuing with familiar, established activities, and can provide an opportunity for sharing and giving. However, creativity does not have to be about an outcome, nor necessarily about doing. A salt dough session with an activity that involves moulding dough into a shape, then kneading it back together to mould into a different shape, without producing a finished article, can be as enjoyable as producing an intricate model that is then baked and painted. Watching a flower-arranging demonstration offers the opportunity to admire a work of art without the pressure of having to produce something. On each occasion, as long as the individuals concerned have engaged in the activity in a way that is satisfying to them, then the activity session is a success.

Many individuals have a creative side, however, their participation in creative activities may be directly affected by their perception of their ability levels. An effective session leader can encourage the individual to participate to a level they are comfortable with – from simply watching to making choices; from working independently to working with the assistance of another. The important factor is that the individual works to a level that they find acceptable. Some individuals will have been exceptionally skilled in particular creative activities; they may be acutely aware of their inability now to achieve their own standards, and may decline to be involved at any level. This is an understandable position that should be acknowledged and accepted.

Activity | **Handicrafts**

Benefits: **These are generally familiar activities, with well established skills – good for hand–eye coordination, sense of achievement, and offering the opportunity for giving.**

Ideas: Knitting, sewing, tapestry, embroidery, lace-making, macramé.

Equipment: Knitting needles, sewing needles, wool, tapestry equipment, threads, material, patterns, cord, beads. Research craft suppliers for equipment aimed at those with difficulties and disabilities – needle threaders, one-handed knitting needles, and ready prepared items that simply need finishing off.

Procedure: Be aware of safety issues for the residents involved in the activity, and other residents in the area. Where possible, use equipment appropriate to skill level (such as large-hole tapestry sheets, large-eyed needles). Where possible, give value to the work – knit for charity, make a gift for a family member, etc.

Hints: Encourage the resident to undertake the activity as much as they can, offering assistance as required. Remember that the outcome is only important if it is important to the resident taking part. If the resident requires a high-standard outcome, then more assistance may be required.

Residents should be offered the opportunity to participate in handicraft activities in whichever way they choose. Being part of a knitting circle provides a sense of belonging, and an opportunity to encourage socialisation and conversation over a shared task – even if the task is never completed!

Speechmark

Activity **Art Clubs**

Benefits: **Often a familiar activity, good for hand–eye coordination. Offer the opportunity for self-expression and communication. Sense of achievement.**

Equipment: Paper, pens, pencils, pastels, crayons, inks, paint, table coverings, aprons, brushes, sponges, stamps, stencils, water. Area for drying.

Procedure: Art sessions can be run in a number of ways:

- *Free sessions*, where residents create whatever they wish to.

- *Themed sessions*, where residents work to an agreed theme (summer time, Christmas, children).

- *Group sessions*, where all the residents work together on a large project.

Objects can be used for decorating – for example, clay pots, plant pots, china plates, glass, plaster objects.

Be imaginative in the use of sponges, stencils, etc – especially if residents have difficulties holding brushes.

Consider displaying completed work, if the resident wishes.

Hints: Be aware of residents who have a tendency of putting things in their mouths.

Have an area to move completed work to, to dry.

For the less able, pre-printed pictures can be used; however, be aware of the risk of offence.

Speechmark

Activity **Flower Art**

Benefits: **Attention, concentration, sense of achievement, self-expression. Good for hand–eye coordination, colour recognition.**

Equipment: Dried or fresh flowers. 'Oasis', paper, glue, scissors.

Procedure: Decide beforehand on the content of the session: this could be collage using flowers; flower arrangements; using dried or silk flowers for decoration. Encourage sensory input during the session – smelling fresh flowers and discussing colours, types, memories of flowers etc.

Ideas: **Collage** – as for painting, collages can be run as free sessions, themed sessions, or group sessions. Ensure that the glue provided will stick the materials available. Protect tables and residents.

Flower arranging – provide each person with a vase or 'oasis' in a pot or basket. Allow residents to select the flowers they would like to use, and where they would like them to go. Where possible, allow the residents to arrange the flowers. However, if necessary, they can be arranged under the resident's instruction, and the resident will still have a sense of achievement.

Decorations – dried and silk flowers can be used to decorate and make a range of items: for example, decorative straw hats (small and large); painted cardboard boxes (small and large); card-based picture frames; handmade cards; laminated bookmarks. Again, ensure that the glue available will stick the materials to be used.

Speechmark

Activity **Salt Dough**

Benefits: **Provides opportunity for self-expression, based around a familiar medium, easy to manipulate and mould.**

Equipment: Pre-prepared dough, rolling pins, cutters, plastic knives, cocktail sticks for making markings, food dye or paint for painting once baked. It will be necessary to have access to an oven to bake the pieces. Dough can be stored, wrapped in a polythene bag, in a fridge.

Procedure: Supply each resident with a piece of dough (moderate size) for them to mould and manipulate in any way that they choose.

Alternatives: Rather than pre-preparing the dough, some of the residents could mix the dough as part of the activity.

Dough shapes can be used as hanging decorations – make a hole in the object before it dries if this is the plan.

New Clay can be used, which is air-drying, however, some residents find this medium too messy in comparison with salt dough.

Recipe: 2 parts flour to 1 part salt, with a little cooking oil. Add small amounts of water to the mixture until it becomes a firm dough. Add food dye to mixture for all-over colouring, or wait until fully dry and then paint.

If baking, do so in a low oven, checking regularly until hard. Alternatively, the dough can be dried out in a warm place (eg, airing cupboard).

Ideas: Christmas decorations, wall hangings, picture frames, bowls, 3D objects, nameplates.

Speechmark

Activity **Gardening**

Benefits: **Self-expression, ongoing projects, enables giving, sense of achievement, sensory-based activity.**

Equipment: Depends on the kind of gardening to be undertaken: pots, raised flower beds, greenhouse, seeds, plants, vegetables, herbs, gardening equipment (adapted equipment can be purchased from suppliers such as Smitcraft and Nottingham Rehab – telephone numbers in Appendix 2), polythene sheets to protect the floor (if need to bring the gardening indoors), gardening gloves, watering cans.

Procedure: Gardening can be undertaken as part of an ongoing project – the group of interested residents could come together as a gardening committee with responsibility for the development of certain areas: a bed within the gardens; a raised bed; the pots around the grounds; or perhaps the hanging baskets. The group could then discuss and agree the plants needed; make a trip out to the local garden centre to purchase the agreed items, and then have a number of sessions planting and maintaining.

Alternatives: Individuals could garden to their own needs – growing and potting houseplants for their individual rooms, as gifts for family members, or for summer fairs and fundraising events.

A greenhouse could be established, so that more able residents could undertake more intensive growing and gardening activities.

Hints: Make contact with local community groups, or interested staff and family members. They might be willing to work alongside residents to develop the gardening club.

Speechmark

Activity **Food-Based Activities**

Benefits: **Familiar activities; sensory-based; self-expression and self-worth; skills maintenance; enables giving.**

Equipment: Ingredients, mixing bowls, weighing scales, measuring jugs, measuring spoons, stirring spoons, cooking trays, aprons. Access to a microwave, oven or hob. Oven gloves, timer.

Procedure: Depends on the activity to be undertaken.

Ideas: Baking cakes, making sweets, making tea and toast, baking biscuits.

Safety: The key concern behind food-based activities is that of safety. For this reason, many facilities would not have resident access to kitchen areas.

Alternatives: purchase a tabletop oven or hob, or make an agreement with the kitchen staff as to times that would be acceptable for cooking items that have been prepared in another area – perhaps the dining room.

If using a tabletop oven or hob, and if using electrical equipment such as kettles and toasters, ensure a risk assessment is compiled and that there is a safe practice policy to work to.

Other health and safety considerations:

■ Staff who run food-based activity sessions should have basic food hygiene awareness.

■ Good hygiene should be maintained among those undertaking the activity (hand-washing, wearing of aprons, cleaning work surfaces).

■ Safe practice should be maintained – thorough cleaning of the equipment used, and avoidance of high-risk food products (such as shellfish, egg and protein-based products).

Speechmark

Activity **Woodcraft**

Benefits: **Familiar activity, sensory nature, good for hand–eye coordination, upper limb strength, self-expression and creativity; opportunity for giving.**

Equipment: Depends on the project to be undertaken. Materials – wood, glue, nails, screws, paint, varnish. Equipment – wood, drills, screwdrivers, hammers, saws.

Procedure: Depends on the project to be undertaken. It is possible to purchase ready-assembled kits from suppliers such as Smitcraft (see Appendix 2), that require a minimal amount of tool use, and so reduce the safety risk, or that require only staining, painting, or varnishing.

Ideas: Footstools, bird boxes, small coffee tables, wood-based models, picture frames, clocks.

Safety: As for food-based activities, woodcraft activities that require the use of equipment with a high risk factor should be thoroughly risk assessed, and a safe practice policy devised.

As mentioned above, it is possible to purchase kits that reduce the level of risk involved.

Reducing the numbers of residents involved in the activity will increase the level of supervision possible, and therefore reduce the level of risk.

Hints: As much as possible, items made should have value – they should be given as gifts, put into use by the resident or by the home (bird tables, for example).

Speechmark

Activity **Door Boards**

Benefits: **As with life-history books, door boards can help memory and trigger reminiscence, they help carers' knowledge of the residents, are fun, and aid communication and self-awareness.**

Equipment: Card, magazines, photos, fabric, scissors, glue, pens, paper, etc.

Duration: This activity may take a number of sessions to complete, with each session lasting as long as the resident wishes to continue.

Procedure: This activity is best carried out on a one-to-one basis. Sit with a resident with the various materials, and using background knowledge of the residents and their response to the materials available to them, design a door board that has meaning to the individual and to which they relate. Attaching the board to a bedroom door can help them relate to the room to which it is attached. Be aware that photographs of the residents can be used, but ensure that the person in the photo is familiar to them – some residents with dementia may not recognise photographs of themselves as an older person, and a photo of them as a younger person would have more meaning.

Hint: This activity is likely to be most appropriate and beneficial for people with dementia. (See 'Life-History Books' [page 52] for a more general approach to gathering biographical information.)

To ensure that the door boards retain value and meaning, this activity may need to be undertaken on a regular basis.

Speechmark

Activity | **Photography**

Benefits:	**Attention, concentration, and self-expression. An excellent method of encouraging sharing for those for whom communication may be difficult.**
Equipment:	Camera, film.
Procedure:	Encourage residents to select photographs that they would like to take. Try to have photographs processed as soon as possible, to aid memory of the activity.
Hints:	Consider having a focus for taking the photographs – a project that the photographs are a part of: collages of favourite things, places, people, a seasonal reflection on spring, summer, winter or autumn.
	This is an ideal activity for the partnership approach – residents can choose the photographs that they would like to have taken, and another can actually take the photograph.

Speechmark

Social activities should be primarily about fun and laughter. They offer the opportunity for developing and reinforcing social relationships between individual residents; between residents and their families, and between residents and staff. They should provide the opportunity for sharing experiences, generating memories, and reinforcing natural, everyday events.

However, it is important to remember that many residents may have spent years alone before moving into a care home, and therefore may be less than comfortable with the idea of socialising with others, particularly when most, if not all, of their companions are strangers. Social activities should offer the opportunity for residents to get to know one another in a non-threatening, non-confrontational manner.

For social activities to be successful, there is a need for numbers. Ensure that all visitors, families and friends are made aware of social events, and reinforce the welcome for them to join in and participate. Consider ways of advertising social events, to ensure that they are clearly brought to the attention of those who might like to participate.

By their very nature, social activities will generally be passive in style – activities that residents can experience and participate in without the need for great physical activities or skill. Consequently, it is possible to have larger groups participating in social activities. So be prepared, with as many helping hands as possible. It is likely that refreshments will be involved, and assistance will be needed to ensure that the event runs smoothly, with all needs met.

Activity **Sing Along**

Benefits: **Can help memory (of familiar songs), fun, communication.**

Equipment: Song sheets, music, a 'confident' voice.

Procedure: If possible, give out song sheets for those who can read; have a familiar range of songs on a tape or CD. Start up the singing and encourage residents to join in. Where possible, encourage residents to identify songs as you begin to play them, or invite residents to select a song to sing. Try to encourage as many people as possible to join in (including staff) – the more the merrier.

Hints: Music will appeal to all abilities and all ages, as long as it is music of choice for the individual. So this kind of activity can involve many residents, with differing needs and abilities, including those with poor speech, who are often able to sing.

Karaoke is proving a popular addition to sing along sessions – the machines often have tapes of either background music to sing along to, or tapes with someone singing to give a strong backing vocal (particularly useful for non-singing activity organisers), and the microphone enables residents with weaker voices to really make themselves heard.

Sing alongs are popular as entertainment sessions, with professional singers both performing and leading the sing along.

Encourage entertainers to include the residents (if they so wish) in the show.

Remember to check out skills among the staff – there may be someone who can sing or play a musical instrument.

Speechmark

Activity **Dancing**

Benefits: **Exercise, memory (of familiar songs, of dancing as a young person), social contact.**

Equipment: Space, music, dance partners.

Procedure: Encourage residents to move and dance, even those who are sitting or who are in wheelchairs. Encourage residents to dance together where possible. The more staff and families that can be involved in this kind of activity, the more dance partners there will be, and the more successful the activity will be.

Alternative: Try a tea dance. Collect together some old favourite pieces of music. Open up the event to families and friends. Encourage the residents to dress in their finest clothes. Prepare a music plan. Announce the next dance, encouraging those participating to take partners and move on to the floor. Support the event with tea and cakes.

Make contact with dance groups and youth groups – residents may enjoy watching others dance, especially if the more able among them can then be invited to take part.

Ideas for dance groups and demonstrations:
Ballet groups, ballroom dancers, line dancers, tap dancers, Scottish or Irish dancers, Morris dancers.

Speechmark

Activity **Animals**

Benefits:	**Reduces anxiety, triggers memories of previous pets.**

Equipment: Owner and registered PAT (Pets As Therapy) pet (not always dogs!). Reputable pet shop owner and pets. Family pets.

Procedure: PAT pets need little input from the activity organiser. On initial visits the owner should be shown around the home, introduced to residents who would like to see the pet; and advised of individuals who are not pet lovers. In future visits, other than arranging suitable times for visits and keeping residents informed of when the pets are coming in, the owners are normally happy to wander the home, taking the pet to the identified residents.

Family pets, as long as they are well trained and behaved, can undertake a similar role.

Pet shops will often put on a display for residents – bringing a range of animals for them to see and pet where appropriate.

Alternatives: Try a pet show. Invite staff, families and visitors to enter their pets into categories of a pet show, with awards for champions.

Invite local youth groups to come along and join in pet sessions – the residents will often enjoy watching the children enjoying the animals.

Contact wildlife centres, urban farms, or open farms to explore the possibility of someone visiting the home with animals such as owls, snakes, pygmy goats, and pigs – either inside or outside.

Speechmark

Activity **Musical Instruments**

Benefits: **Coordination, communication, and self-expression.**

Equipment: Range of instruments, such as tambourines, triangles, hand symbols, maracas, bells, bongos, hand drums. Music with a good beat.

Procedure: Place the instruments within reach of the residents, and then put on some music. Encourage the residents to select an instrument if possible; alternatively select an instrument for them that they are likely to be able to play. Encourage the residents to respond to the music using the instruments.

Alternatives: Consider setting up a band or a choir with a group of residents. The group would require careful selection, to ensure that the abilities are complementary.

Try hand chimes. They are relatively easy to play and can generate a fabulous sound with a little preparation, guidance and practice.

Musical instruments can be expensive to purchase; however, it is worth spending that bit extra on quality instruments, for ease of use, quality of sound and usually good aftercare. It may be worth checking with local schools or music groups if they have secondhand equipment that could be purchased more cheaply.

Speechmark

Activity **Refreshment-Based Activities**

Benefits: **A purely social event that can be accessed by all ability levels.**

Equipment: Crockery, cutlery, coffee, tea, sherry, wine, fruit juice, squash, cheese, biscuits, cakes, – according to the session to be undertaken.

Procedure: Invite residents to attend the session; include an open invitation to families to join in (if appropriate), and then serve refreshments as required. Background music can be useful to generate a social atmosphere, although this should be kept low to enable discussion and conversation.

Alternatives: Have the event on a rolling basis; keep the group small, and invite carefully selected residents (based on shared backgrounds, likes, and interests) via personal invitation cards to a room that is not often used (small quiet lounge, for example). Use crockery that is different from that used on a day-to-day basis – to give the event an air of being 'special'.

Hints: Offer different groups the same opportunity, to ensure fairness.

Social gatherings such as coffee mornings can be used as fundraising events, and as informal residents and relatives meetings to discuss ideas for future activities, and comments and concerns about the home.

Speechmark

Activity **Cinema Show**

Benefits: **Social event, can aid attention span and concentration, and reminiscence.**

Equipment: Video player and a range of videos. Refreshments – drinks, popcorn, icecream.

Procedure: Encourage the resident group to select the film to be watched. Ensure that the video player is working and the room is set up so that the film can get underway promptly. Ensure that residents are aware of what film is playing, where, and the start time. Agree with the group beforehand the arrangements for taking a refreshment break(s).

Alternatives: Try to access a screen and projector to give a feel of being in the cinema, or arrange an outing to the local cinema for the real thing.

Hints: Providing a full range of videos is necessary, if sometimes difficult. Encourage staff and families to lend videos from personal collections (ensure their safekeeping), to increase the range available.

Include: classic films, operas, ballets, short piece films, musicals, and video footage of memorable events.

Be prepared, so that if questions are asked about the videos – the storyline, the actors, or the events portrayed – then background information is available.

Be aware that video clubs will often not provide membership for organisations, and take care when planning a large group viewing as this may be prohibited without a licence. Read the opening credits of any video for clarity.

This page may be photocopied for instructional use only. *Group Activities with Older Adults* © Vicki Dent 2003

Speechmark

Activity **Outings**

Benefits: **Provides the opportunity to access community facilities and resources; offers the opportunity for more everyday activities.**

Equipment: Depends on the outing to be undertaken; however, as a basic guide: transport, staff, first aid equipment, personal care equipment, blankets, umbrellas, pager, mobile phone or phonecard, breakdown organisation contact details.

Procedure: Outings present an organisational challenge. It is always worth checking out any venues beforehand, to ensure that disabled access is available to the areas that the residents wish to visit (do not rely on literature to give the full picture). Decide beforehand on the object of the outing – a drive, a pub lunch, a visit, shopping – and communicate this to all involved. Decide on how residents will be selected for the outing – rota, first come, first served. Complete a risk assessment for the outing, once the residents have been identified, to highlight the care needs that may be required during the outing, and therefore the staff assistance needed on the outing.

Hints: If access to a vehicle is not available, investigate the following options for hire or loan: community transport schemes; dial-a-ride schemes; wheelchair accessible taxis or minibuses; local organisations – Red Cross; St John Ambulance; multiple sclerosis societies; Parkinson's disease societies; hospice organisations; social services or local council groups, disabled schools or organisations; local undertakers (they often have minibuses that they will hire out at a very reasonable cost).

Speechmark

Activity Entertainment and Parties

Benefits: **Opportunity for social contact; passive-type activity, therefore accessible to all.**

Equipment: Space, keyboard or piano (although many artists will bring their own equipment), refreshments. Other equipment may be necessary, depending on the nature of the event – eg: somewhere to change; fancy dress (should be optional for residents); music for a party; decorations.

Procedure: Decide on the nature of and reason for the event – theme or no theme, celebration, or just a general event. Identify budget available. Book entertainment in plenty of time, particularly at popular times of the year (Christmas, New Year, Valentine's Day, Burns' Night).

Advertise the event – to staff, residents, and families. Consider refreshments to be made available – drinks, cakes, biscuits, buffet – and make arrangements with kitchen staff. Enlist help from staff and volunteers – the more help there is, the greater the number of residents that can be enabled to participate. Identify the venue for the entertainment or party, and prepare the area in plenty of time: a place for the entertainer; seating arrangements; access arrangements; decorations. If the entertainment is to be in the evening, ensure that night staff are aware of a possible change to any usual routine.

Alternatives: Try to consider a full range of entertainers, rather than just sticking to old favourites. Try speakers, slide shows, magicians, theatre groups, dancers, musical recitals, and pantomimes as well as the traditional singers. If the staff group are enthusiastic and creative, it may be possible to put on a regular in-house show.

Speechmark

Activity **Bingo**

Benefits: **Hand–eye coordination, concentration, attention, memory, number recognition, upper limb movement.**

Equipment: Bingo cards that residents can see easily; method for marking off numbers – dry wipe pens, counters, buttons; caller's kit – board of numbers, numbers; prizes (if required).

Procedure: Give each resident a card (or more than one if they wish), and a means of marking off numbers (pen or sufficient counters). Ensure that everyone is seated in a place that they can hear and can receive assistance if required. Take a number from the pool (a bag, bingo machine, or bowl) and announce the number pulled, allowing time for residents to confirm the number and check the card before moving on. Place the called numbers on a board, or mark off called numbers for double checking as required. Games can be played in a number of ways – winner of a line (any line, or a specific line); winner of four corners; winner of two lines; winner of a full house. Prizes can be allocated or selected as available.

Alternatives: Bingo kits can be expensive to buy but are easily made. Bingo cards should be large print. If small ones are available, they can be enlarged on a photocopier; or you could design and draw them out on A4 paper, then laminate them so that they can be reused. Bingo boards can be drawn out, and the numbers can be made.

Traditional bingo games include the numbers 1–90. This can be adapted to have a lower range of numbers for ease of checking and to increase the speed of the game.

Bingo games can be adapted away from numbers. A musical bingo game is available, so is a reminiscence bingo. The musical bingo includes a tape of songs, and the boards have song titles rather than numbers. As the tape is played, residents need to identify the song and then check to see if the title is on their card, marking off as usual if it is. The reminiscence bingo has an item or name associated with each number. As the number is called the item is also called which can generate discussion around the item. Picture bingo can be devised with everyday items, and as the picture is drawn, residents can identify the item and then check off their card as usual.

Activity **Fairs and Fetes**

Benefits: **Social opportunity, fundraising opportunity, fun.**

Equipment: This will depend on the nature of the fair or fete, but is likely to include: space (indoors or outdoors), people, stalls, products, entertainment, games, refreshments, adequate parking.

Procedure: This is an activity that is best organised via a committee, due to the amount of work involved. Planning for this kind of event should start in plenty of time, with an agreed purpose. Decide on a date; the range of stalls; people to contact; tasks to be undertaken; and then have regular review meetings to monitor progress along the way.

Ideas: Summer fetes, Christmas fairs, garden parties.

Stalls: book, cakes, bric-a-brac, sale of work (that residents have made in creative sessions), plants, tombola, raffle, guess the weight, guess the name, guess the amount.

Refreshments: drinks, ice-cream, barbecue, strawberry teas, doughnuts.

Games: hook-a-duck, sponge throwing, darts, tin can alley.

Other: face painting, bouncy castles.

Information stalls for local associations and groups: Alzheimer's society, Parkinson's disease society, Red Cross, St John Ambulance, police, fire brigade, Territorial Army.

External stalls: craft, jewellery, clothes. (A charge could be made for having a stall, or take a percentage of the profits.)

Speechmark

For many residents, verbal communication will be difficult, and can lead to people becoming withdrawn and out of contact with their environment and surroundings – particularly those with a cognitive impairment. Sensory activities are one way of trying to engage people who have withdrawn, and can open up communication routes. Sensory activities may also be useful for those who are in the later stages of life; who are being nursed in bed; who are low aware, and who show little response to everyday stimulus.

It is generally understood that sensory activities can be used for relaxation purposes, but they can be equally effective in making contact and engaging a resident, and therefore care should be taken not to overstimulate. Sensory activities will obviously address the main range of senses – sight, sound, smell, touch and taste. To avoid overstimulation, sensory sessions should be limited to one or two senses at a time, and careful monitoring for signs of wellbeing is required.

Sensory activities do not need to be limited to multi-sensory environments. Although many care homes are beginning to explore the possibility of providing this kind of room, many more do not have the space for such facilities. This need not exclude sensory activities from the programme. Such activities will often be offered on an individual basis, and are best done in a quieter area – perhaps in an individual's room. However, some sensory activities can be offered on a group basis, adapted to meet the different needs of residents wishing to participate.

Activity **Rummage Box**

Benefits: **Sensory experience to aid communication, engagement, contact and awareness.**

Equipment: Plastic storage box containing a variety of 'sensory' pieces incorporating sounds, colour, texture, smell. For example – fabric, coloured paper, buttons, shells, 'toys' that vibrate or make noise, tumble tubes, pine cones, lavender bags, feathers, koosh balls.

Procedure: Depends upon ability level – invite the resident(s) to rummage; offer single items to individuals to handle; or actively enable the individual to experience the sensation by placing objects in their hands, or passing feathers under their chin for example.

For the more able residents, open up a discussion about the object – the experience and any memories that might be triggered.

Alternatives: Have a dressing-up box, that residents can rummage through, with gloves, scarves and hats of different styles and fabrics.

Have jars and boxes of items that need sorting, such as buttons, stamps, shells, wool, coins, pens, brushes, feathers – this will encourage rummaging as well as sorting activities.

Hints: Be aware of residents who may have allergies to different fabrics, or who show signs of dislike of certain sensations (feathers, for example). Also, be aware of residents who like to collect things: activities could be disrupted, and residents distressed, by other residents taking items away. Finally, remain aware of residents who may have a tendency to put items in their mouths.

Activity | **Fruit-Tasting**

Benefits: **Sensory input, communication route. Suitable for all ability levels. May aid reminiscence. Potential health benefit for those with limited appetite.**

Equipment: A variety of fruit – some complete, some chopped and prepared into small pieces for eating.

Procedure: Invite more able residents to look at and handle complete fruit pieces to discuss what they might be, where they come from, the range of fruit available, favourite fruits, fruit experiences – growing, picking. As the discussion progresses, arrange for the fruit to be cut up for tasting, offering residents the opportunity to do so, if able. Invite the group to taste the different fruits, commenting on the tastes, and likes and dislikes. Include other residents in the area who were not involved in the original discussions by taking fruit to them. Be aware of residents who have swallowing difficulties, of those with diabetes, or who have food intolerance, or are on special diets.

Alternatives: This format can be followed with a range of other food and drink products, such as crisps, cheeses, breads, cakes, doughnuts, jams and spreads, and the range of teas, coffees, or fruit juices.

Hints: Ensure that other staff are aware of the activity session – kitchen staff may be willing to make up different tastes, or could alert the activity organiser to a surplus of fruit to prevent wastage.

Speechmark

Activity **Hand Massage**

Benefits: **Communication route. Reduces anxiety and agitation. Improves skin condition and circulation. Relieves stiffness and arthritic pain. Be aware of sensitive skin – especially where there is paralysis following a stroke, for example.**

Equipment: Alcohol gel, wet wipes or warm flannel for cleansing skin. Massage oil, hand cream or talc, as preferred by the resident. Towels to protect clothing. Pillow or cushion on which to rest arm.

Procedure: Ascertain from the resident that they wish to have a hand massage – for those with no verbal skills, watch for signs of displeasure (such as pulling away).

Put a towel over the resident's lap, support the arm on a pillow or cushion. Cleanse the hands of the giver and receiver. Using oil, cream, or talc, place a small amount in the palm of the giver and rub hands together to warm. Hold the resident's hand palm down and begin by stroking the hand to pass the oil, cream, or talc on to their skin. Massage the wrist bones, then the back of the hand, then each finger. Turn the hand over, and massage the palm. Turn the hand over again, and continue to massage the back of the hand. Circle the wrist to increase movement. Stroke the hand to finish. Do not rush. Some residents like to return the compliment by massaging the carer's hands – allow this to happen.

Hints: Do not use aromatherapy oils unless trained to do so. Scented hand creams are acceptable, as long as there is no skin reaction, and encouraging residents to smell the cream can enhance the sensory element of the session.

Group Activities with Older Adults © Vicki Dent 2003

 Speechmark

Activity **Smell Quiz**

Benefits:	**Mental stimulation – to work out identity of smell; communication; fun; reminiscence; discussion.**
Equipment:	Everyday ingredients with a strong, preferably recognisable smell – for example, coffee, curry powder, lavender, peppermint essence. Jars for holding the ingredients. (Bowls or plates could be used; however, the more open the receptacle, the less intense the aroma and the increased level of difficulty – particularly for those whose sense of smell has diminished.)
Procedure:	If possible, group the residents together, and invite someone to have first go at sniffing an ingredient in the jar to see if they can identify the ingredient through smell. The colour and texture may give additional clues if required.
Alternatives:	This could be run as a competition to see how many ingredients people can guess correctly, or as a sensory experience with open discussion as to whether it is a nice smell, and what memories it brings back. In this case, correct identification would not be important.
Hints:	Be aware of personal preference – some residents will be sensitive to certain smells; watch for any signs of dislike, and withdraw any items that cause offence. However, smelling something that is strong or unpleasant will not necessarily cause an unhappy response. It will simply be an alternative stimulus.

Speechmark

Activity **Feely Bags**

Benefits: **Sensory stimulation, mental stimulation, object recognition, communication, and fun.**

Equipment: Plastic bags, cardboard boxes, large ice cream tubs – things that are not see-through; that residents can put their hands into comfortably, filled with packing material: for example, polystyrene pieces or shredded paper. Place from five to seven familiar objects in the container among the packing material.

Procedure: Invite residents to take turns in feeling in the container, finding an object, and then trying to identify the object without looking at it.

Hints: For less able residents, place only one object in the container and see if they can find it and identify it, either by name or by purpose. If the packing material causes confusion, then the activity can be undertaken without it.

For residents without speech, but with good understanding, pictures of the objects within the container can be put on a board for them to indicate the object they have found. In this case decide beforehand how many guesses an individual can have.

Alternatives: Fill a number of containers with materials of different sensations, rather than a range of everyday objects. For example: cotton wool, feathers, rice, dried pulses, shredded paper. Discussions can then focus on whether the sensation is a pleasant or unpleasant one, as well as attempting to identify the contents.

This page may be photocopied for instructional use only. *Group Activities with Older Adults* © Vicki Dent 2003

Speechmark

Activity **Music**

Benefits: **Sensory stimulation, self-expression, communication – suitable for all resident groups.**

Equipment: Live or recorded music, musical instruments.

Procedure: There are a number of different ways of using music within an activity programme. For each kind of session, ensure that residents are aware of the role of the music in the session, and attempt to provide for the wide range of music interests of the resident group.

Ideas: *Music for relaxation:* Use music in the background to enhance the mood for relaxation (see pages 105–112 on meeting emotional needs, for more detail on relaxation activities). Be aware that music is a personal thing – music that may be relaxing for one person may not be for another.

Music appreciation: Take a theme for the session – a particular style of music (jazz, classical, modern, 50s, country and western), or a particular artist or composer, and present a compilation of music based on the theme. Encourage residents to select the theme and, if possible, to contribute particular tracks to the compilation. Gather background information on the style, artist, etc to offer information to the residents alongside playing the music.

Music quiz: Compile a selection of recognisable songs; play the opening bars of each track, and see if residents can identify the song. Often residents will sing along to the song, either as an alternative to guessing the title or as well as guessing it. This is easier to do if the compilation is on CD, as many CD players have the facility for playing the opening 15 seconds, and are then easier to reset to the beginning of the track.

Hints: Avoid making assumptions about individuals' taste in music – often residents like to hear more recent music, certainly from the 1960s and some enjoy hearing current music, in order to be able to converse with younger grandchildren.

See also: Musical Instruments, Entertainment and Parties, pages 67 and 71.

Activity Complementary Therapies

Benefits: **Sensory stimulation, relaxation, reported health benefits – reduces stiffness, pain, anxiety, and stress; aids sleep, circulation and waste elimination.**

Equipment: Qualified practitioner, quiet area with supportive furniture (bed, recliner chair, couch), towels, cleansers, oils (for massage).

Procedure: This activity should only be undertaken by someone with a professional qualification. Weekend 'taster' courses are not sufficient training

Therapies: Massage, aromatherapy, reflexology, Indian head massage.

Training: Complementary therapy training is normally offered by most adult education centres, and generally takes an academic year to complete. Costs vary, but are likely to be in the region of £150–180.

Therapists: Complementary therapies are increasing in popularity, with the result that qualified practitioners are more available, and many are willing to come into care homes to undertake treatments. Some points to consider if this is a desired:

■ Check qualifications and insurance levels

■ Agree a safe practice of work – obtaining medical approval (from GP) prior to treatments commencing.

■ Agree method of recording treatments offered.

■ Understand contraindications and effective communication systems.

Speechmark

Activity | Multi-Sensory Environments

Benefits: **Sensory stimulation for relaxation, or stimulation.**

Equipment: Dedicated area (can be a separate room, or an area within a room that can be screened or curtained to provide a dedicated area). Specialist equipment.

Note: Having established a multi-sensory environment, it is essential that staff wishing to use the area have received guidance and training on the use of the equipment and the running of a multi-sensory session.

Procedure: As with all activities, some residents will enjoy the multi-sensory experience, others will not. Thorough knowledge of the person is vital before introducing them to the multi-sensory experience. The staff involved in providing the session must be aware of signs of both good and adverse reactions for that individual. They must be aware of the resident's likes and dislikes regarding music and touch. They must have a good relationship with the resident, and be able to communicate as much as possible with that individual.

When a resident is first introduced to the multi-sensory equipment, it should be on a one-to-one basis; the session should be short (unless there are very obvious signs of pleasure); individual pieces of equipment should be introduced one at a time, switching off equipment that is not in use. Good observation skills are required to monitor residents' responses to the individual pieces. Any signs of dislike should be acknowledged immediately, and that piece of equipment withdrawn. It is not unusual for residents to interact with only one or two pieces of equipment during a session.

Records of each individual's response to the multi-sensory equipment must be kept. Following a multi-sensory session, observations should be maintained and recorded to ascertain the longer term effect of sensory stimulation. Before providing repeat multi-sensory sessions, the member of staff should familiarise themselves with any after-effects of the previous session, and should make a judgement as to the appropriateness of further sessions. Multi-sensory sessions should not be repeated in the same day; however, observation of the effects of sensory input will indicate how often is appropriate for each individual.

This kind of activity is offered specifically to boost an individuals' sense of wellbeing and self-esteem, and therefore is likely to be offered on an individual basis.

The majority of the other activities featured in this book should also create wellbeing and consequently increase feelings of value and worth, by either direct or indirect means, depending on the skill of the activity organiser. The more involved, occupied and engaged an individual feels, the more likely they are to have a greater sense of wellbeing. The skilled activity organiser will create failure-free activities, and that accompanying sense of achievement will boost feelings of value and esteem.

However, on occasion there may be the need to offer some very specific attention, to boost an individual's esteem level. For example, if a resident has been unwell and is in need of an extra boost; for a new resident who is feeling unsettled and anxious, or for a resident who has little contact with either family and friends or the group programme.

The range of activities that can be offered within this category is as wide as the range of interests of the resident group. Anything that an individual particularly enjoys and would especially enjoy on an individual basis can be included – for example, shopping trips, reading, playing board games, doing jigsaws. As these kinds of activity have been included in more detail under other activity types, they will not be repeated here. This section includes activities that can boost self-esteem, and that are not covered in other sections.

Activity Health and Beauty (Make-Up)

Benefits: **Self-awareness, self-esteem, maintenance of personal care standards.**

Equipment: Make-up (preferably belonging to the individual); brushes (essential if make-up is to be shared); cosmetic mirrors.

Note: For reasons of hygiene, nothing should touch the skin of more than one resident without it being cleansed between residents.

Procedure: Sit with the resident, either individually or in a small group (if acceptable to the members of the group). Where possible, arrange residents so that they can view themselves in a mirror. Encourage the resident to select the make-up that they would like to wear, and how they would like to wear it. If possible, enable the residents to apply the make-up for themselves.

Hints: This activity should be undertaken at appropriate times of the day – for example, applying make-up towards the end of the day, shortly before a resident begins to consider retiring for the night, reduces the value of the activity.

For many residents, wearing make-up will have been an essential part of their preparations for the day, and they would not have shown themselves to the outside world without powder and lipstick. This should be known to as many staff as possible to ensure that make-up is applied during morning personal care routines. For others, make-up will not have played a role in their life, and this could be an inappropriate activity to introduce now – unless specifically requested by the resident, of course.

Speechmark

Activity Health and Beauty (Hair)

Benefits: **Self-awareness, self-esteem, maintenance of personal care standards.**

Equipment: Combs, brushes, hairdryer, rollers, styling products.

Procedure: Ideal activity following a bath, when hair is likely to be wet and easy to care for. Dry and style as desired by the resident.

Hints: Many care homes have access to a hairdresser who will take responsibility for more technical hair care, such as cutting, styling, or perming. However, there may be periods of time between hairdressing appointments when residents would welcome the opportunity to have their hair done. As many people will testify, if you have been unwell or feeling a little low, then having your hair done can generate a sense of wellbeing.

Of course, hair care does not have to be restricted to female clients.

Speechmark

Activity Health and Beauty (Manicures)

Benefits: **Self-awareness, self-esteem, maintenance of personal care standards.**

Equipment: Nail files, nail clippers or scissors, hand-cream, nail polish, nail polish remover, cotton buds.

Procedure: As with hair care, this activity does not have to be restricted to the women.

The activity organiser may undertake a part or a full manicure, depending on the resident's request and the care policy in the home,

Remove any existing nail polish, and soak the hands in a bowl of warm water, aiding relaxation as well as softening the nails for cutting. Clean under the nails using a nailbrush, and dry the hands well. Cut the nails with scissors or clippers, taking care of delicate skin areas around the nail bed. File to shape, and then offer a coat of polish if appropriate. Complete the manicure by rubbing handcream into the skin.

Hints: Take care when cutting the nails of individuals who have diabetes – if the skin is nicked, there is an increased risk of infection.

Nail polish is a very personal thing: some residents will have worn it regularly; others never. Respect residents' experiences.

A range of colours should be available, and residents should be encouraged to make a choice. For those who are unable to make a choice, and there is an agreement that varnish is appropriate, then be aware of making appropriate choices on the resident's behalf.

Speechmark

Activity **Family Trees**

Benefits: **Self-worth, self-value, information-gathering and sharing, communication.**

Equipment: Access to information – library, internet. Scrapbook or photograph album for recording information.

Procedure: This is an activity that would be applicable to only a small group of residents with interest in gathering family tree information, and the ability to recall family information.

An ongoing activity that involves tracing back family links, recording births, marriages and deaths, alongside other useful information about the family history.

Hints: This activity is best carried out with input and information from family members, as a group project. The information can then be used to aid memories for the individuals concerned.

It may be worth considering looking to volunteers for this kind of activity – perhaps students of history or journalism could be enlisted to undertake the sessions with residents: to do the research and compile the information. This work, along with that of life-history work, could be developed into biographical pieces, especially for those with important or famous links and histories.

See also Life-History Books, page 52.

Speechmark

Activity **Biographies**

Benefits: **Self-awareness, self-esteem, aids reminiscence, self-worth.**

Equipment: An individual with skills and time to write individual biographies.

Procedure: Residents will have had a lifetime of experiences, and will have fascinating stories to tell of the changes they have seen, the roles they have undertaken and the experiences that have shaped their lives. A skilled writer could work with the resident to compile a biography for personal pleasure, or for publication.

Hints: This activity is one that must be undertaken on an individual basis – not all residents will wish to tell their stories, and both the resident and their families must be fully involved in agreeing the overall aim of writing the biography.

Useful contacts such as colleges, universities, writers' guilds, and publishers should be able to recommend journalists or writers who may be willing to come in; to sit with the resident, to hear and then write their stories.

Some residents may have both the ability and the desire to write their own biographies, and consideration should be given to accessing equipment such as word processors, typewriters, and personal computers that can be set up for the individual to use.

See also Life-History Books, page 52.

Speechmark

Activity **Roles**

Benefits: **Self-awareness, self-esteem, self-worth, self-identity.**

Equipment: Depends on the role to be undertaken.

Procedure: Identify roles within the home that could be undertaken by individuals or groups of residents. For each role, undertake a risk assessment related to a particular resident undertaking that role. A risk assessment should consider the potential risks, the likelihood of each potential risk occurring, and then the actions that should be taken to minimise or eliminate the risk.

Residents who express a desire to have a role within the care home could then discuss the kind of roles available to them, and the level of responsibility that they could take on, based on the findings of the risk assessment and the abilities and capabilities of the individual resident.

Ideas: The following is a list of roles that could be undertaken. Some have been explored in more detail in other sections of this book. The list is by no means exhaustive:

- Domestic chores – laundry, setting tables, drawer-tidying

- Pet and plant care

- Hospitality roles

- Production of a newsletter

- Assisting with food preparation and service, including refreshments

- Assisting with administration tasks – word processing documents; delivering mail or newspapers to residents

- Bingo caller or quiz master

- Assisting with shop trolleys or library trolleys

- Guest speakers – many residents have interesting experiences they could share, for example slide shows of travels, or talks about previous occupations

See also Educational and Employment Activities, pages 113–119.

Speechmark

Activity Intergenerational Activities

Benefits: **Self-awareness, self-esteem, self-worth, self-value.**

Equipment: Depends on the activity to be undertaken. A group of willing youngsters from schools, colleges, or youth groups.

Procedure: Many residents will feel valued and respected if they have the opportunity to share their skills and experiences with younger generations. This can be achieved in a number of different ways; however, before these ideas can be implemented, a relationship with youth groups, nurseries, schools or colleges will be necessary. Contact should be made with the group leader or teacher, and clear guidelines established as to how work is to be undertaken; what resources will be necessary, and which organisation will take responsibility for what.

Ideas: Listening service – residents could work with younger children from local schools, acting as 'listeners' for children to practise their reading skills. The resident and the student should build up a regular relationship to help the child feel comfortable. The residents involved will need to have good hearing and be able to correct the child where necessary

Grandparent role: many youngsters today are without a close grandparent. Residents could build up a 'surrogate' grandparent relationship, through regular visits by the children to the care home. Activities could be organised for the children to undertake, with the residents assisting the children – ball games, art sessions, baking sessions, for example.

See also Lifelong Learning, page 117.

Speechmark

The residents' spiritual needs will be extremely varied. For some, spirituality may have played an important role in their lives – one that they are keen to continue. For others, religion and spirituality may have become important only recently, and for others, religion and spirituality will hold no interest at all.

It is important to be aware that spirituality is more than religion alone. Residents may not wish to worship, but may wish to have time with someone from a particular faith, to read certain writings or to spend time in contemplation or prayer. The key, as always, to providing spiritually-based activities, is to know the interests, desires and needs of the resident group.

The frequency of spiritual activities will also be dictated by the residents. For some, a recognition of holy days such as Easter, Christmas, or Passover will be enough; for others, a monthly service will meet their needs; for some, there may be a request for individual worship.

On admission of a resident, it is important to ascertain their religious faith and their need for spiritual activity. In many homes there is a core of people from a similar faith, and arrangements are likely to be in place to meet their needs. However, there may be residents who move into the home with an alternative faith, and then research is required to meet their needs – for example identifying local resources for providing worship or individual contact, and exploring customs of that faith.

Activity **Bible Reading and Prayers**

Benefits: **Remain in contact with spiritual interests and needs.**

Equipment: Bible(s).

Procedure: Sit with the resident, either individually or in a small group, and read small extracts or prayers from the Bible. Wherever possible, encourage residents to select, and if possible to read, the passages.

Hints: If providing this activity for a group of residents, be sure that all individuals within earshot are happy to listen to the readings. It may be necessary to hold this kind of group session in a quiet lounge, or individually, in a resident's own room.

Alternatives: Members of the particular faith from the local community, or family members, may be willing to come in to hold a Bible-reading or prayer session with residents.

Some residents will enjoy Bible-reading sessions as an activity in their own right; others will prefer to have the Bible-reading as part of a larger activity, with perhaps hymn-singing and prayers as well.

Identifying passages and prayers relevant to certain times of the religious year will be important background work for the activity organiser to undertake, as many residents of long-standing faith will expect to hear specific readings on specific occasions.

Speechmark

Activity **Hymn-Singing**

Benefits: **Remain in contact with spiritual interests and needs.**

Equipment: Music, songsheets.

Procedure: Many residents will have a good memory for hymns, so encourage them to select hymns to sing. Provide music and songsheets to help those who may not have an accurate memory of the hymn.

Hints: As with Bible reading, ensure that those within earshot of the session are happy to hear the hymn-singing.

Alternatives: As with Bible reading, residents may enjoy hymn-singing as a specific activity; others will prefer it to be part of a larger activity.

Members of local congregations will often be happy to come in on a regular basis to lead a hymn-singing session, usually bringing a number of people to add their voices, and often bringing musical instruments such as guitars and keyboards to add to the atmosphere of the session.

At Christmas time, residents of the Christian faiths are likely to enjoy carol concerts, and making contact with schools and churches will often provide access to a choir who may be happy to come into the home.

Hymns do not have to be restricted to worship activities or hymn-singing sessions; often residents will request favourite hymns during general sing along sessions.

Speechmark

Activity **Services**

Benefits: **Remain in contact with spiritual interests and needs.**

Equipment: Worship books, music, keyboard.

Procedure: Many homes arrange for individuals from different faiths to come into the home to lead a service on a regular basis. The activity organiser is then responsible for arranging the room and gathering the residents, and the service leader will generally bring along any other equipment required – for example, candles, items for communion. Some services may include singing, and a keyboard and player may be required.

Hints: When making arrangements with the local clergy, it is often useful to plan a programme of services rather than attempting to plan on an *ad hoc* basis, as the clergy's diary often fills quickly and the residents may be disappointed.

Many services may need to be held during the week to accommodate the clergy.

Alternatives: Some faiths will have lay preachers who are willing to come in to run services on a regular basis.

For residents who do not require a regular service, there may be a need for special services around the high days and holidays of each faith. Again, input to these by local ministers will need planning in advance.

Some residents may have been members of a local place of worship for many years, and would prefer to continue their attendance there, rather than attend services within the home. This should be accommodated as far as possible, and making contact with members of the local congregation may identify volunteers to provide transport for the resident.

Activity **Visits**

Benefits: **Remain in contact with spiritual interests and needs.**

Equipment: Volunteers.

Procedure: Residents may prefer to receive visits from members of their own faith for individual worship, readings, or practices. Make contact with the local group of the resident's faith; make it known that the resident would like to receive regular visits, outlining the purpose of the visit, and request input from the faith community.

Hints: This kind of individual activity is best undertaken in the resident's own room, to allow privacy and respect for the individual's customs.

Alternatives: Some faith leaders may be willing to offer individual input to a number of residents, and will arrange a regular visit day when they can visit a number of individuals during a visit.

Speechmark

Activity | Contemplation Time

Benefits: **Remain in contact with spiritual interests and needs. Exploration of individual spiritual needs.**

Equipment: None.

Procedure: Residents may wish to have time made available for spiritual contemplation. This kind of activity could be undertaken by the volunteers or clergy who come in to visit, or by staff within the home, and may or may not have a religious focus. In later stages of life, many individuals like to have time to consider their past; to undertake longed-for activities; to make amends; to re-establish contacts, and to establish a plan surrounding their wishes in death and burial.

This kind of activity is likely to be best undertaken on an individual basis; however, there may be the desire among a small group of residents to hear from certain organisations regarding, for example, living wills, burial styles, or processes for final wishes, bequests, or donations, and this could be run on a group basis. Under these circumstances, careful consideration must be given to the setting for the session, to avoid upset or distress to others who may not wish to partake in such discussions.

Speechmark

Activity Religious Discussion Groups

Benefits: **Remain in contact with spiritual interests and needs; opportunity to explore belief issues with others.**

Equipment: Volunteers of similar beliefs to lead discussion session.

Procedure: Visiting volunteers or members of religious groups may like to take the opportunity to run religious discussion groups for, or with, residents. There may be a local group in the community who meet on a regular basis to discuss beliefs and issues relevant to their faith. These groups could be invited to hold their discussion meetings in the care home, to enable residents to participate. Alternatively, their meeting information could be sent to interested residents, and then arrangements could be made for residents to attend the meetings, as desired.

Another possibility would be for a group of residents in the care home, who would like to have a regular discussion group of their own, to be facilitated by a resident, a member of staff, or a volunteer from the local community.

Hint: It is important that the discussion group leader is informed of the values and beliefs of the religion that forms the basis of the discussion group, in order that the session is run in an informative and considerate way.

Group Activities with Older Adults © Vicki Dent 2003

Speechmark

Activity Celebrations

Benefits: **Remain in contact with spiritual interests and needs.**

Equipment: Depends on the nature of the celebration.

Procedure: Most faiths have a diary of religious and spiritual celebrations, and festivities that practising residents may wish to observe. Some of these celebrations require specific equipment, or that particular processes or rituals be followed. Activity organisers should ensure that they are informed of the religious needs of the resident groups; make contact with the different faith leaders, and have an arrangement with those faith leaders in order that celebrations and festivities can be observed.

Hints: Activity organisers should seek to obtain faith calendars that list the dates for different celebrations and festivities. Many good yearly diaries list the main events at the front of the diary, for information.

Speechmark

In terms of activities, the word 'cultural' is used in the broadest sense to identify activities related to artistic and aesthetic interests, as well as those pertaining to particular cultural groups.

Understanding the cultural, religious and social backgrounds and histories of a particular group of residents is important, in order to retain links with the local communities, and to be able to provide traditional, long-standing, familiar activities.

Given the mobile nature of young people, it is not unusual for staff to be working in regions other than those in which they grew up. Therefore, they may be unaware of local traditions, so time taken to research the background and interests of the local area will be invaluable.

Consider the lifestyles and recreational pastimes of the resident group. Did the working lives of the adult population centre around work? Is the area affluent, and perhaps the ladies spent time undertaking charity and voluntary work? Is it an area of unemployment? Have people had few resources to undertake many recreational pastimes? Is the experience of the residents' leisure time one of pubs and clubs, or one of theatres and dining out? As the picture develops, so residents' cultural and traditional needs will become clearer; however, remember that interests and tastes can change; residents may well appreciate the opportunity to find out about and experience different cultural and traditional kinds of activities.

Activity | **Theme Events**

Benefits:	**Links into community events; fun; recognises family and community traditions.**

Equipment: Depends on the event, but is likely to include food, refreshments, entertainment, decorations, games, costumes.

Procedure: Identify a calendar of events based around themes of interest, and discuss with the resident group methods of celebrating. Depending on the size of the event, this kind of activity may be best organised and arranged through a committee of willing people.

Ideas:

- A celebration of a certain period of time – for example, 1950s night, 1920s day, Victorian event

- Use of an event as the theme – Royal Ascot, Wimbledon

- Local traditions –for example, ceilidhs

- National days (UK) – Saints Andrew, George, Patrick, David

- National days (international)

- Chinese New Year

- Colour themes – for example, black and white theme

- Other themes – theatre, horror, nursery rhymes, films.

See also Entertainment and Parties, page 71.

Speechmark

Activity **High Days and Holidays**

Benefits: **Links into community events; fun; recognises family and community traditions.**

Equipment: Depends on the event, but is likely to include food, refreshments, entertainment, decorations.

Procedure: Identify a calendar of high days and holidays. Discuss with the residents the days that they would like to recognise and celebrate, and agree the nature of the celebrations. Plan in advance, and give invitations to families and friends as appropriate.

Ideas:
- Burns' night

- Valentine's Day

- Mothers' Fathers' and Grandparents' day

- Easter

- May Day

- Bank holidays

- Passover

- Chinese New Year

- Jewish New Year

- Halloween

- Bonfire night

- Christmas Eve, Christmas Day

- New Year's Eve, New Year's Day

- Royal birthdays, weddings, and anniversaries.

Speechmark

Activity **Cultural Events**

Benefits: **Addresses the artistic and aesthetic interests of residents.**

Equipment: Depends on the style of the event.

Ideas: *Art and craft exhibitions:* Invite residents to produce art or craft work that could be featured in an exhibition. This could be held in the home, or contact the local art gallery, library or museum to see if they would be willing to host the exhibition. If held outside the home, arrangements would need to be made to advertise the event, and to arrange access for interested residents to visit.

Theatre trips: Make contact with local theatres to identify the programme of events, the access for disabled people, and the discounts available for tickets. Advertise the programme to the residents, and arrange visits accordingly.

Museum and gallery visits: As for theatre outings – explore the programme available, and arrange as interests require.

Recitals: As for exhibitions, this kind of activity can be an internal event with residents preparing, and then offering pieces for a recital (music, readings) to which other residents, staff and family are invited. Recitals can also be external events, with residents attending programmes run by local groups as desired.

Speechmark

Activity Round-the-World Trip

Benefits: **Social interaction; increases awareness of different cultures; encourages reminiscence.**

Equipment: Depends on how seriously this session is taken. To undertake it in its fullest sense, there will be a need for an aircraft soundtrack; costumes for a pilot and stewards; a steward's trolley, and a range of country-related 'props', such as maps, music, food and drink.

Procedure: Set up the room as if it were the inside of an aircraft, with chairs in rows, a central aisle, and a 'cabin' at the front. Identify individuals to undertake the roles of pilot and steward(s). If possible, put up posters from the different countries to be visited on the walls. Once the residents have taken their seats, run the soundtrack of the plane taking off; get the pilot to offer a commentary regarding the route being taken, and then 'arrive' at the first destination. The steward(s) can then take the trolley round with a selection of food and drink from the country that they have 'landed' in. Having local music playing will add to the general atmosphere. While 'landed', encourage residents to share their experiences of visits to the country. When everyone has had time to share, then invite the residents to settle back for the next part of the journey, and repeat the process of 'taking off', commentary, trolley run and discussion. Attempt to identify travel experiences of residents who may attend prior to the session, so that countries of relevance can be included.

Speechmark

Activity Introduction to Cultures

Benefits: **Retain and reinforces cultural identity; encourages information on different cultures; encourages reminiscence, social interaction, and fun.**

Equipment: Depends on the event to be organised, but is likely to include food and entertainment from different countries; a slideshow; costumes.

Procedure: Identify the different cultures represented by residents and staff within the care facility as a starting point. Alternatively, through a discussion session, identify cultures that residents have had experience of, or would like to know more about.

Invite individuals (residents, staff, or outside contacts) who are representative of or knowledgeable about the different cultures to be explored, to lead the session.

Arrange for local costumes to be made available for people to wear or see. Arrange for locally available traditional food and drink for residents to try. Arrange for traditional entertainment and music. It may be possible to have an individual lead a slide show, showing photographs of the country, and to lead a discussion around the traditions of different cultures.

Ideas: Try to link this kind of activity to a day of relevance to a particular culture – for example, an Irish event on St Patrick's day, with perhaps an Irish flavour to the main meal; some Irish dancing by children in traditional dress, followed by an afternoon slide show of some of the places to visit and sights to see in Ireland.

Speechmark

As mentioned in previous chapters, moving into a care facility can bring with it a huge range of emotions – many positive, as people settle and become more content; but equally, some negative, such as anger, guilt, sadness, anxiety and fear.

General activities can go a long way towards alleviating some of the negative emotions. For example, encouraging people to become involved in the community of the home may allay some fears and anxieties; enabling people to continue with hobbies and interests will provide familiarity and comfort. On occasion, however, some activities are required to focus specifically on reducing negative emotions where possible. These activities, as with those that boost self-esteem, are likely to be offered on an individual basis, although they should not be excluded as ideas for group activities as well.

It must be remembered that some of the more serious negative emotions, including depression, may well require input from external professionals, such as qualified counsellors, psychiatric nurses or doctors.

Activity   Pets as Therapy (PAT) Pets

Benefits: **Petting animals has been shown to aid relaxation and bring about emotional comfort; encourages wellbeing through familiarity; can aid reminiscence and communication.**

Equipment: Registered Pets as Therapy (PAT) animal and owner.

PAT pets are registered because of their temperament and behaviour. They are usually well trained and very accustomed to being patted and being among vulnerable people – those in wheelchairs or with walking aids.

Procedure: Many PAT owners become regular visitors with their pets (not always dogs), and once they have established a routine with the home, need little input from the activity organiser, being happy to visit the home and move around without staff in attendance (if appropriate for the resident group).

Hints: Having made contact with a local PAT owner (see Appendix 2 for national telephone number) then the PAT owner will arrange a convenient time to visit with the pet. Prior to the visit, it will be useful to establish with residents who would like to meet the pet, and whether there are any residents who have a fear or dislike of animals. This information can be shared with the PAT owner on their first visit, and they can be introduced to those who would like to meet the pet, as well as being helped to identify those who would not.

See also Animals, page 66.

Speechmark

Activity **Advocacy**

Benefits: **Provides the opportunity for an individual to share thoughts and concerns with an independent person, who can then represent their views on their behalf. Especially useful for residents with limited access to family members.**

Contacts: Informal advocacy is the role of all staff – acting as the voice for residents, and ensuring fair and adequate service provision. However, more formal and effective advocacy must be provided by individuals who are independent of the home. There are a number of organisations that have been established for the purpose of offering advocacy, and that have experience in this field. Some of these organisations are condition-orientated: for example, The Alzheimer's Society, the Parkinson's Disease Society, the Stroke Association. Others are more general organisations, such as Age Concern, Help the Aged, and community health councils.

Procedure: If a resident indicates a need for an independent person to represent their concerns, then they should be provided with information on organisations and contacts, but where possible the resident should make an appointment themselves. It may be necessary to invite a number of individuals from a range of organisations to visit the resident, so that they may meet them and then make a choice of advocate accordingly.

Speechmark

Activity **Befriending**

Benefits: **A more informal form of support that will benefit residents who have limited community support from family and friends. May be of particular benefit to residents who participate in few group activities.**

Contacts: Many of the organisations that offer advocacy services may be willing to offer a befriending service, however, befrienders are more often volunteers.

Procedure: Make contact with volunteer organisations, such as Community Service Volunteers (CSV), Volunteer Bureaus, Red Cross volunteers, League of Friends groups, or alternatively advertise within the local community for volunteers to support the home.

Arrange with potential befrienders to spend time with the residents, to get to know them, so that the resident may indicate their enjoyment (or otherwise) of the contact with the individual. If both parties are comfortable with the contact, then initially facilitate regular contact between resident and befriender; over time, the relationship will develop, and input from the activity organiser will be unnecessary.

Hints: Volunteers can undertake many roles within a care home; however, effective recruitment, support and monitoring procedures are required. Volunteers will have access to vulnerable people, and their recruitment should include an application form, references and criminal records disclosure, as if they were being employed. Regular support and supervision is essential if the volunteer is to feel a valued member of the team. Roles and responsibilities should be clearly outlined, so that potential volunteers are aware of the commitment required of them, and to avoid any confusion once they start.

Speechmark

Activity **Relaxation**

Benefits: **Can reduce stress and anxiety; generate increased feelings of wellbeing; promote sleep, and improve concentration.**

Equipment: Quiet area without distractions; comfortable chairs; blankets for those who feel the cold (body temperature can drop during relaxation); music; relaxation routine.

Procedure: Ensure that everyone who wishes to join the relaxation session is present, as this is an activity that is best undisturbed. Ensure that everyone is comfortable, and can hear. Ensure that the residents understand the purpose and nature of the relaxation session.

Select a routine – relaxation sessions can be based around breathing exercises, physical movements or psychological imagery and meditation. A relaxation routine could include a component of each of the three styles.

A fairly traditional relaxation routine is included in Appendix 7.

Hints: Music can be played at the end of a relaxation session, to enhance the effect; however, be aware of different tastes in music – what one individual finds relaxing to listen to, others may not.

Alternatives: Relaxation sessions can feature within other activity sessions, particularly exercise sessions, as a useful cool-down activity, and in multi-sensory sessions, to aid the relaxation effect of the multi-sensory environment.

Some more able residents may like to try their hand at yoga – an exercise form that encourages stress relief and relaxation. However, this is best taught by a qualified yoga instructor.

This page may be photocopied for instructional use only. *Group Activities with Older Adults* © Vicki Dent 2003

Speechmark

Activity | **Support Groups**

Benefits: **Provides opportunity for information- and idea-sharing; brings together individuals with common concerns; can provide emotional support.**

Procedure: Support groups are normally formed around a common theme, perhaps a condition or a circumstance. They should have an agreed format, including frequency and purpose of meeting, and benefit from having a consistent group leader or facilitator.

If the purpose of a support group meeting is to aid knowledge- and information-sharing, then inviting external people to come and speak will be both interesting and useful to the group. If the group's primary focus is support for its members, then more support will be gained if relationships can develop, keeping new faces to a minimum.

Hints: Support groups in care homes may take the form of residents' meetings, providing the opportunity to discuss ideas or concerns about the activities of the home; or of relatives and residents' meetings, where residents and relatives can come together for a social or information purpose.

Community support groups may be available for residents and their relatives to attend, such as The Alzheimer's Society groups.

Speechmark

Activity **Family Contact**

Benefits: **Maintains continuity with relatives and informal carers; retains roles and identity; increases feelings of self-worth, value and esteem.**

Equipment: Depends on the activity undertaken.

Procedure: This kind of session will need to take into consideration the needs of the family. Many families are happy to come into the care facility to visit, joining in with their relative in general day-to-day activities. Others will find this more difficult, but will still wish to have active involvement with their family member.

Ideas: *Home visit:* With the agreement of the care team, the resident and the family arrange a home visit for the resident. This may require a member of staff to stay with the individual, or may simply involve providing transport. Be considerate of the longer term effect that this may have on the resident, with regard to possible distress caused by having to return to the care facility.

Family lunch: Arrange a separate sitting at a meal time for the resident to be able to invite their family to come and join them for lunch – perhaps a Sunday lunch. Again, this may require a staff member to be with the resident, or it may require organisation and serving of the meal only. Alternatively, it may be possible for the resident to go out for lunch with their family.

Outings: Many families, particularly spouses, miss the opportunity to go out with their loved ones to a social event, such as a tea dance; to visit a place of interest, or the cinema or theatre. Encourage family members to join their relative on a home outing; alternatively, arrange for an individual outing for the resident and their family.

Speechmark

Activity | **Individual Activities**

Benefits: **Increases sense of self-worth; improves self-esteem; addresses very specific needs of the individual.**

Equipment: Depends on the kind of session to be undertaken. Time.

Procedure: This can be a very time-consuming approach to take; however, on occasion there will be a very real need on the part of the resident for individual, tailor-made activity input.

Talking, whether about issues of concern or generally, is the most obvious individual input. However, almost any activity can be offered on an individual basis, in the resident's room, in the main communal areas, or out of the home.

Individual activities include:

■ Playing cards, dominoes, board games, jigsaw puzzles

■ Reading newspapers, a magazine, books, poetry, letters

■ Word games, crosswords, quizzes, word searches

■ Writing letters, compiling life stories or biographies for the individual

■ Providing a hand massage, manicures, or hair and beauty session

■ Playing musical instruments, or listening to music

■ Sensory input, including smell quizzes, feely bags, image projectors

■ Outings, whether into the garden or out into the community

■ Art and craft work – painting, drawing, collage-making, salt dough, card-making.

Speechmark

Many residents express a desire to continue with employment-type activities – those that they perceive to be of a work nature. This may be out of a desire to continue to be worthwhile, as they encourage a sense of self-identity, and a feeling of being useful, and promote feelings of self-worth. This desire may also be generated out of a lack of acceptance or understanding of their need to be in a care facility. For people with dementia, work-type activities are often familiar, and are based on routines that they feel able to continue with successfully.

For many, the opportunities to go out to work from the care home will be limited. However, there are work-type activities that can be offered within the activity programme. These may be provided on an individual or group basis, and on a planned or *ad hoc* basis (as and when the resident wishes to undertake the activity). Some of the work-type activities will have an inherent risk. Good risk assessment should ensure that the activity could be provided once all reasonably practicable steps have been taken to reduce the level of risk.

Bear in mind that consideration should be given to other peoples' perception of work. Some residents may have undertaken very high-powered work roles, and their desire may be for work-type activities of a similar nature. Others may never have worked, and may show little interest in work-type activities. Attitudes of families and staff members should also be addressed, to ensure a clear understanding of the purpose behind offering work-type activities.

Educational activities are included in this section. Obviously, all activities have the potential to be educational – learning to knit; learning a new card game; undertaking salt dough for the first time; however this section looks at activities that are included specifically as an educational tool.

Activity | **Domestic Chores**

Benefits: **Many residents, particularly (although not exclusively) women, miss the very familiar domestic chores that will have played a large part in their lives, and they may appreciate the opportunity to have a role in undertaking this kind of 'activity' again. Such a role can enhance self-esteem, reinforce self-identity and generate feelings of wellbeing and satisfaction.**

Equipment: Depends on the kind of 'chore' to be undertaken.

Ideas: *Laundry:* Gather together familiar kinds of plastic or wicker laundry baskets, and a range of laundry items, such as towels, sheets, tablecloths, and spare clothes. Invite the resident(s) to help with the laundry. Ask them to sort or fold the items in the basket. Work together to encourage communication and role-modelling.

Setting tables: Using the usual tableware, such as table mats, knives and forks, salt and pepper pots, flowers, and napkins, invite the resident(s) to help lay the tables. Ask them to select what to lay next, to encourage object recognition and appropriate sequencing. Work together to complete a table, but try to allow the resident to lay their own area without correcting mistakes (this can be done discreetly after the resident has moved away). Try to ensure that this activity is provided near to mealtimes, to validate its value as well as acting as a prompt for mealtimes.

Dusting: With a duster and polish, invite the resident(s) to help with the dusting. Ask them to choose an area for cleaning – dining area, bookshelves, etc. Work together, chatting about their own memories of housework, or any other topics that they may offer for discussion. Be aware of physical tiredness; offer breaks from the 'work'.

Drawer tidying: Wherever possible take a drawer that is used for everyday storage, either in the lounge area or in a resident's bedroom. If this is not possible, then a container of items for tidying (knives and forks, and napkins) will work just as well. Invite the resident(s) to help with the tidying, enabling them to undertake as much of the task as possible.

Plant and pet care: Encourage interested residents to take responsibility for the care of plants or pets, such as cats, birds and fish. Plant care will include regular watering, feeding and maintenance. Pet care will include feeding and cleaning of cages or tanks.

Hint: If a number of residents are interested in taking on this role, then care should be taken to avoid over-watering or over-feeding.

Brass cleaning: Brass-cleaning may be a familiar activity for some, so having the opportunity to clean brass from around the home may be welcome.

Speechmark

Activity **Hospitality Club**

Benefits: **Increased sense of self-worth and self-esteem; encourages relationship-building, particularly with new residents; offers the opportunity for visitors to hear about the home direct from the residents.**

Procedure: Care homes are notoriously busy places, with many visitors coming and going. More able residents could take on responsibility for meeting, greeting and making welcome certain visitors. While this might not apply to regular visitors, those who make arrangements to look around the home – whether visiting professionals, potential residents and their families, and new residents – could be met by the 'hospitality club'.

Hints: It might be useful to have the activity organiser or another member of staff as a member of the hospitality club, to ensure that someone is on hand to answer any specific questions, and that any welcome event runs smoothly.

Alternatives: If a meeting and greeting committee is not appropriate for the home, then the 'hospitality group' could have the responsibility for organising a welcome event, such as a coffee morning, for new residents or new staff.

Activity **Newsletter**

Benefits: **Provides an opportunity for communication, both within and outside the home. For those who take a role in developing the newsletter, there is cognitive stimulation, an increased sense of self-worth and value, and an opportunity to be part of a finished outcome.**

Equipment: Word-processing facilities; printing and copying facilities, and resources for information and news features.

Procedure: Agree beforehand the style and frequency of the newsletter. These can be time-consuming, so it may be better to start with a low-frequency issue that could be published more often as the newsletter and interest becomes established.

Encourage contributions from residents, staff and families – developing a newsletter independently can be difficult to sustain. Recruit residents to take on roles – for example, provider of crosswords or word games; provider of horoscopes; provider of local interest stories; typist (particularly if a resident has computer skills and a computer); editor; proof-reader; copier; collator; distributor.

Hints: Residents may not be able to take an active role in the production of a newsletter but they will always be a source of information and news stories – celebrations of birthdays or anniversaries, biographical columns around peoples' past histories; reminiscence materials and memories.

Speechmark

Activity **Lifelong Learning**

Benefits: **Cognitive stimulation; concentration; memory; communication; sharing skills and knowledge; learning new skills and knowledge.**

Procedure: There are many organisations looking at lifelong learning and ways of encouraging older people to undertake new learning and development for themselves, or to participate in the learning and development of others.

Contacts such as the University of the Third Age, the Dark Horse Venture, Age Exchange and Age Resource, as well as local adult education colleges and intergenerational groups, will be good places to start when looking to provide learning and development opportunities.

Youth groups and schools or colleges will often have learning opportunities that older people could assist with – acting as a 'listener' for people learning to read; 'historian' for those studying past events; 'tutor' based on existing, well-established skills.

Hints: Many local authorities have specific funding to support lifelong learning initiatives, which may be worth exploring to help cover costs of equipment such as computers, and costs of tutors, etc.

Speechmark

Activity **Speakers**

Benefits: **Cognitive stimulation; opportunity for interaction, communication and discussion; opportunity for learning and development.**

Equipment: List of speakers; equipment required by the speaker – slide show projector, overhead projector.

Procedure: Identify with the resident group the kind of speaker and the kind of topic they would find of interest. Identify suitable speakers – residents, families and staff may be willing to lead a session; alternatively, contact local organisations for speakers' details or lists. Ensure that the speaker is made aware of the resident group that will make up the audience – in particular, their levels of attention and concentration in order that the talk can be tailored in style and length. Ensure that the event is well advertised, particularly if the speaker is an outside person who may be making a charge. Provide equipment to ensure that all can hear – microphone attached to a karaoke machine, or linked into a hearing-aid loop system. Provide refreshments as part of the activity.

Useful organisations to contact for speakers include:

Women's League; Women's Institute; Probus groups; University of the Third Age; local-interest groups; relevant organisations and associations, such as Alzheimer's Society, Parkinson's Disease Society; welfare organisations; animal welfare organisations.

You could also contact interesting individuals – for example, the mayor or Pearly King (interesting because of their role), an owl expert, bee-keeper, or hatmaker (interesting because of a hobby).

Speechmark

Activity **School and College Links**

Benefits: **Retains sense of self-worth and self-identity; provides opportunity for learning and development, and for sharing of skills and knowledge.**

Equipment: Depends on the link or activity to be undertaken.

Procedure: Explore possible links with local schools and colleges, with regard to ways in which residents might be able to support students in their studies, or alternatively ways in which residents might be able to undertake studies of their own.

Ideas: *Care facility as a learning centre:* Many adult education colleges run evening classes, and they may be willing to hold the class in the care facility (if appropriate). This would enable residents to attend the evening classes alongside people from the local community, without the need for transport or staff time to facilitate this. Often the colleges themselves have student support services, so that an individual can have additional resources to help them undertake written work, for example. Alternatively, the college may be willing to provide the services of a tutor to run a session, or a series of sessions, with residents. Often, the college meets the cost of the tutor, through lifelong learning funding, and the care facility needs to meet only the costs of any materials.

Distance learning: Many organisations now offer distance learning as an option. Residents with a particular interest may wish to undertake study in this way, with support offered by the college. Note that this may have equipment implications, such as computer or internet requirements.

See also Intergenerational Activities, page 90.

Speechmark

Appendixes

1 Background Information

Resident's name _____ **DOB** _____

Preferred name _____ **DOA** _____

Background information

Place of birth _____

FAMILY

Mother _____ Father _____

Siblings _____

Significant events – early years _____

_____

_____

Occupations _____

_____

_____

Relationships _____

_____

_____

FAMILY

Partners _____

Children _____

Friends _____

Significant events – later years _____

_____

_____

Hobbies and interests _____

_____

_____

Activity likes and dislikes _____

_____

Future activity plans _____

_____

Background Information

(continued)

Resident's name _____

Date of assessment _____

Physical

Mobility	☐ Independent	☐ With assistance	☐ Immobile
Dexterity	☐ Full	☐ Some	☐ Minimal
Paralysis	☐ None	☐ Some	☐ Complete

Intellectual

Concentration	☐ Good	☐ Limited	☐ Poor
S-T Memory	☐ Good	☐ Limited	☐ Poor
L-T Memory	☐ Good	☐ Limited	☐ Poor
Understanding	☐ Good	☐ Limited	☐ Poor

Sensory

Hearing	☐ Good	☐ Limited	☐ Poor	☐ Wears hearing aid
Sight	☐ Good	☐ Limited	☐ Poor	☐ Wears glasses

Speech

Level	☐ No difficulties	☐ Very quiet	☐ No speech
Content	☐ Lucid	☐ Sometimes confused	☐ Generally confused

Challenging behaviour

Wandering or Aggression	☐ No	☐ Sometimes	☐ Yes

Other   ☐ Epilepsy   ☐ Diabetes

Name of assessor _____

Signature _____

Speechmark

2 Telephone Contacts for UK Resources

Catalogues

Speechmark	01869 244644
Rompa	0800 056 2323
Nottingham Rehab	0845 606 0911
Smitcraft	01252 342626

Training in exercise for the elderly

Extend	01263 825670
Health Education Authority	0207 383 3833

Focus on elderly

Age Concern England	0208 679 8000
Counsel and Care	0207 485 1550
The Dark Horse Venture	0151 729 0092
The Institute of Human Ageing	0151 794 5062
NAPA	0207 383 5757
Help the Aged	0207 253 0253
University of the Third Age	0207 737 2541
Research into Ageing	0207 404 6878
Centre for Policy on Ageing	0207 253 1787

Animals

PAT Scheme for Dogs	01732 848499

Relatives and Carers

Relatives Association	0207 916 6055
Carers National Association	0207 490 8818
Royal Air Force Association	0208 994 8504

Reminiscence

Age Exchange	0208 318 9105

Condition-based

Alzheimer's Disease Society	0207 306 0606

(ADS also coordinates the Network of Dementia Services Development Centres.)

Sensory difficulties

RNIB	0207 388 1266
Partially Sighted Society	01302 323132
Talking Newspapers Association	01435 866102
Talking Book Service	0208 903 6666
National Listening Library (B)	0207 407 9417
Action for Blind People	0207 732 8771
RNID	0207 296 8000

Activity related

Council for Music in Hospitals	01932 252809
Horticultural Therapy (Thrive)	0118 988 5688
Live Music Now	0207 730 2205
British Wheel of Yoga	01529 306851

Speechmark

Resident Feedback Questionnaire

The home is currently completing a review of its social activity provision and we would welcome your views.

Completed forms may be returned to the Home Manager or the Activity Organiser

Thank you for your time and your comments.

Do you believe the social activity programme meets your needs?

(or the needs of your relative if you are not a resident) ☐ Yes ☐ No

Please state your reasons:

_____

_____

_____

_____

_____

_____

Would you like to see other social activities within the home? ☐ Yes ☐ No

If yes, please detail your suggestions:

_____

_____

_____

_____

_____

Are there any other comments you would like to make about the social activity programme within the home?

_____

_____

_____

_____

_____

_____

_____

_____

_____

_____

Speechmark

Residents' Participation Record

ACTIVITY AND DATE	INTERNAL ACTIVITIES							EXTERNAL	
NAME									

Speechmark

Activity Ideas and Suggestions

5

Physical activities

Yoga groups	Hydrotherapy	Floor games	Ball games
Walks	Parachute	Swimming	Darts
Sports	Horse-riding	Movement to music	Skittles
Balloon games	Croquet	Carpet bowls	Trips to leisure centres

Cognitive activities

Discussions	Debates	Board games	Talks
Quizzes	Crosswords	Word games	Library
Newspapers	Magazines	Life-history books	TV and radio
Reminiscence	Jigsaws	Memory games	Dominoes
Card games			

Creative activities

Craft sessions	Art sessions	Salt dough	Sugar crafts
Gardening	Cooking	Flower arranging	New clay
Cake decorating	Basket-weaving	Photography	Painting
Drawing	Collage work	Knitting	Sewing
Tapestry	Rug-making	Woodcrafts	Music, drama
Creative writing	Model-making	Collecting	Needlecrafts
Jewellery-making	Papier mache	Craft demonstrations	

Social activities

Sherry afternoons	Coffee mornings	Afternoon tea	Bingo
Wine-tasting events	Beer festivals	Theme events	Entertainment
Card clubs	Beetle drive	Cinema trips	Sporting links
Video evenings	PAT dog visits	Outings	Shopping trips
Visitors	Musical events	Charades	Pet shows
Links with local clubs	Reminiscence	Barbecues	Treasure hunt
Tea dances	Links with schools and	Flower shows	Pub visits
In-house shopping	youth groups		

Sensory activities

Rummage box	Smell quizzes	Feely bags	Music
Food-based activities	Seasonal foods	Taste quizzes	Flowers
Fabrics and textures	Hand massage	Aromatherapy (if qualified)	

Speechmark

5 Activity Ideas and Suggestions
(continued)

Esteem activities

Beauty care	Manicure and pedicure	Hairdressing	Biographies
Foot spa	Hand and foot massage	Charity work	Life stories
Family-tree tracing			

Spiritual activities

Visits from clergy	Services	Visits to church	Bible readings
Hymn-singing			

Cultural activities

Theme events	High days	Holidays	Provide for individuals'
Museum visits	Exhibitions	Theatre visits	cultural needs

Emotional support activities

Access to local	Advocacy	Befriending	Relaxation
support groups	PAT dogs		

Educational and employment activities

Domestic chores	Hospitality club	Newsletter	Local colleges
Open University	Local library	Distance learning	Speakers
Talking books	University of the Third Age	Dark Horse Venture	Employment agencies
Sheltered work placements			

Speechmark

Word Games and Quizzes

Word expansion

Take a large word; write it on a flipchart or board, and encourage residents to make as many smaller words as they can with three letters or more. Give a target for the group to reach. This can be done with residents working individually for a sense of competition, or together as a group.

Hangman

Encourage a resident to come up with the name of a famous person or place. Ask them to share the name with the activity organiser only. The organiser should then put the name on a flipchart as a series of dashes, with each dash representing a letter in the name. Leave spaces between dashes to represent a new word. Residents then suggest letters that might be in the name. If the letter suggested is in the name, this should be written in its respective place. If the letter suggested is not in the name, then a single component of the hangman diagram is drawn. The aim is to guess the hidden name by suggesting one letter at a time before the hangman drawing is completed. A completed hangman drawing is as follows:

Alphabet game

Take a selection of topics, such as girls' names, place-names, fruits – three is usually plenty and can be suggested by the residents. Then take a number of letters – four or five is usually enough and, again, can be suggested by the residents. Then, either individually or as a group, residents need to come up with a word for each topic beginning with the letters suggested. For example, if the topics are girls' names, places and fruit, and the letters are A, T, M, O, R, then the residents need to come up with a girl's name beginning with A; a place beginning with A, and a fruit beginning with A, and so on. To introduce an element of competition, a point can be given for each correct answer, and two points can go to any answer that no one else gave.

This page may be photocopied for instructional use only. *Group Activities with Older Adults* © Vicki Dent 2003

Word Games and Quizzes *(continued)*

Word quizzes

Many of these quizzes have been collected from activity organisers over time, and should not be considered as my own creations. There are also many more quizzes in a range of publications available from Speechmark, high street bookshops and supermarkets. These are a few favourites:

- *Anagrams:* Anagrams are easy to devise, and are best themed – for example, famous people's names, places, colours, items of clothing, girls' names, boys' names, food items.
- *Abbreviations:* Again, collections of well-known abbreviations are easily compiled, although sometimes accurate answers need a little research.
- *Proverbs:* Another popular quiz – to guess the remainder of a given proverb. Residents are often very good on proverbs, and may be able to provide some of the questions.
- *Song titles:* Provide the opening lines of a song, or the chorus, and see if residents can guess the song title.
- *Famous pairs:* Give the residents the name of one half of a famous pair, and see if they can guess the missing partner.
- *Geography quiz:* Using a large-scale map of either the UK or the world, place numbers on the map, and see if residents can guess the place indicated by each number.
- *Mother and child:* Give a type of animal, and see if residents can guess the correct name for their offspring.

Word Games and Quizzes *(continued)*

Colour quiz

There is a colour in every answer:

1 A place for rearing plants and shrubs?   *Greenhouse*

2 Woman attaching herself to a man for gain?   *Gold-digger*

3 Exclude from a private club?   *Blackball*

4 Children's television programme, also a flag   *Blue Peter*

5 Tropical virus?   *Yellow fever*

6 A type of bone fracture?   *Greenstick*

7 Woman having great learning?   *Bluestocking*

8 Country now called Ghana?   *Gold Coast*

9 Worker who defies a strike?   *Blackleg*

10 Jason went in search of this?   *Golden fleece*

11 A piece of land kept free of development?   *Greenbelt*

12 Cowardly?   *Yellow*

13 Write on it with chalk?   *Blackboard*

14 Notorious spot for accidents?   *Blackspot*

15 Wild hyacinth?   *Bluebell*

Word Games and Quizzes *(continued)*

Find the proverb

1	Copper canny, gold silly.	*Penny wise, pound foolish.*
2	The tortoise and the hare.	*More haste, less speed.*
3	The hands have it with a bulb.	*Many hands make light work.*
4	One and one can cause trouble.	*It takes two to make a quarrel.*
5	The court card loses out.	*Jack of all trades, master of none.*
6	Half the stuff of life isn't bad.	*Half a loaf is better than none.*
7	She equals the distance.	*A miss is as good as a mile.*
8	Keeping an eye on it doesn't help.	*A watched pot never boils.*
9	Little ones with eyes not ears.	*Children should be seen and not heard.*
10	Have or have not.	*You can't have your cake and eat it.*
11	He's up for breakfast.	*The early bird catches the worm.*
12	Immediate action saves time.	*A stitch in time saves nine.*
13	Think before making a decision.	*Look before you leap.*

Speechmark

Real money

Can you make all these clues add up to £32. 18s. 5½d.?

			£	s	d
1	A stone	14 pounds	14		
2	Two policemen	coppers			2
3	A bicycle	penny farthing			1¼
4	A musical (with Tommy Steele)	half a sixpence			3
5	A man's name	Bob		1	
6	A singer	tenner	10		
7	A kind of pig	guinea	1	1	
8	A leather worker	tanner			6
9	A monkey's leg joint	ape knee			½
10	The Sun, the Moon and Pluto	3 far things			¾
11	50 per cent of panties	half a knicker		10	
12	To hit repeatedly	pound	1		
13	An unwell sea creature	sick squid	6		
14	A royal head-dress	crown		5	
15	A girl's name	penny			1
16	A popular name for a budgie	joey			3
		TOTAL	32	18	5½

NB: There are 12d to a shilling

Speechmark

7 Sample Relaxation Routine

Begin by making sure everyone is comfortable, warm and can hear. Turn the lighting down low, or off if acceptable to the group, and talk through the routine as follows:

1 Take a breath, breathing in through your nose and out through your mouth.

2 And again, in through your nose and out through your mouth.

3 Now start with your shoulders. Raise your shoulders up towards your ears; feel how uncomfortable that is; hold it; hold it, and relax; let your shoulders drop, and feel how much better that is.

4 And repeat shoulders up to your ears; hold it and relax; let them drop.

5 Now think about your hands. Make a fist, both hands together if you can; hold it; hold it, and then release.

6 This time, lift up your arms in front of you, and make a fist again. Try to tense your whole arm; hold it; hold it, and then let your arms drop into your lap, and let your fingers go.

7 This time, spread your fingers wide; feel the tension in your hands; hold it; hold it, and let go; let your hands drop back into your lap.

8 Think about your back against the chair. Try to push back against the chair; hold it, and relax.

9 And again, push your back against the back of the chair; hold it, and relax.

10 Now think about your bottom. Try to clench your bottom together; make yourself lift up in your seat; hold it, and relax.

11 Let's try that again. Clench your buttocks together, and then relax.

12 If you can, put your knees together, then try pushing them against each other; really push your knees against each other; hold it, and relax.

Speechmark

13 Let's try that one again. Push your knees together, against each other; hold it, and relax.

14 Now let's think about your feet. Try to point your toes away from you, and feel the tension in your feet; hold it; hold it, and relax.

15 This time try to point your toes to the ceiling. Feel the tension in the back of your leg; hold it, and relax.

16 Finally, push your feet against the ground; hold it; hold it, and relax.

17 Now close your eyes and relax for a minute. Think about a place you like to be, perhaps sitting in the garden with the sun on your face. (Some relaxing music can be played during this stage.)

18 Now open your eyes and take another breath, in through your nose and out through your mouth.

19 Thank you everybody.

Speechmark

8 Resident Response to Activities

DATE	PROGRESS SUMMARY	SIGNATURE

Resident's name _____

Sample Weekly Programme

9

This programme is based on a provision of Monday to Friday during the day. Additional activities could be included at the weekend and in the evenings, resources allowing.

Monday	Tuesday	Wednesday	Thursday	Friday
10am Individual room visits.	10am Individual room visits.	10am Individual room visits.	10am Individual room visits.	10am Individual room visits.
11am Gentle exercises in the quiet lounge.	11am Musical quiz in the main lounge.	11am Handicrafts in the main lounge.	11am Skittles tournament in the main lounge.	11am Handicrafts in the main lounge.
11.45am A review of the newspapers and a glass of sherry before lunch in the main lounge.	12 noon Library trolley will be doing the rounds.	12 noon A quick crossword before lunch in the main lounge.	12 noon Shop trolley will be doing the rounds.	12 noon A quick crossword before lunch in the main lounge.
1.30pm Art Club in the conservatory.	2pm Entertainment in the dining-room. 'The Fabulous Four' will be singing your favourite requests.	1.30pm Prize bingo in the dining-room.	1.30pm Minibus outing to the garden centre to select the plants for the hanging baskets and patio tubs.	1.30pm Baking in the dining-room.
3pm Monthly service in the quiet lounge.		3pm Cards and dominoes in the quiet lounge.		3pm Doughnut tasting in the quiet lounge.

137

Index of Activities